WITH LOVE, *Anne*

WITH
LOVE,

Anne

A MEMOIR

ANNE FRIESEN

Ageloff Books
New York City

*I dedicate this book with love
to the memory of my late husband,
Dietrich Friesen.*

And to our dear children, grandchildren and great-grandchildren, all of whom I love and cherish with my whole heart.

I pray that you will accept the message of love this book expresses, for I present it in all humanness and humility, in awe of God's guidance throughout the 80 years of my life.

Contents

Contents

CONTENTS

Foreword

To remember is an act of love. It reflects gratitude for life, for others, and for God. Anne Friesen has carried out this act of remembering by writing these memoirs and poems, and she allows us the privilege of retracing her journey with her. Not only do we travel with her, but she gives us entry to her soul, from which good writing comes.

Anne, who loves life, is passionately involved with life, with people. She also loves words and good language. The result is that she chooses the best words, those that hold energy and accuracy, for her recording. And by doing so, she not only gives us her memories, but she gives us art. Anne's writing reaches high; it awakens us and moves us to our own experiences, that true test of art.

A vital element is Anne's strong sense of place. Her

memory allows her to return to houses and landscapes of her past with a dedication to detail and the associated emotions—a stairwell, a path to school, the particular light through a window. This love of place is connected to her hunger for beauty. Her passion for music and beautiful things combines with her lively memory into a longing for that final beautiful place to which she is going.

Anne joins all those in human history who have left markings of their life journeys, those valuable documents which give us and future generations the necessary perspective and courage for our own lives. That her life has essentially spanned the 20th century is of significance, holding as it does the drama of huge changes in Russia and that eventual power struggle with the democratic West. Anne's narrow escape from starvation and imprisonment in 1920s Russian and the open arms of Canada for immigration is a story that reaches beyond her to us all. Her story becomes our story, and we recognize in the joys and trials of her life how they intertwine with a history that in some way is also ours. Without her words, we might fail to see that.

But those of us who knew her, who are part of her family, have our own memories to which she is inextricably bound. Anne's acts of love—as mother, grandmother, great-grandmother, sister, aunt, cousin, friend—are her finest gifts. It is clear that her love for God, her faith in Jesus Christ, is the burning center of these repeated loving actions. Anne is a bright star glowing steadily in our night sky. These words will keep her glowing for generations to come.

Jean Wiebe Janzen
February 1997

Preface

$\mathcal{I}$ began these memoirs out of a desire to let my children, grandchildren and great-grandchildren know something about my life during what people my age call "the good old days," even though at the time of my beginning, times were anything but good.

My homespun story begins in 1917 in Russia, continues through Canada, moves on to Kansas, and finally reaches the present in Fresno, California. I attribute the journey of my life to the goodness and grace of God who has paved the way with blessings more than I could ask or imagine.

"Now to Him who is able to do immeasurably more than we ask or imagine, according to His power that is at work within us, to Him be glory in the church and in Christ Jesus throughout all generations for ever and ever!" (Ephesians 3:20, 21)

Amen.

Acknowledgments

THIS book was written over a long period of times, and I owe thanks to all who encouraged and helped me in this venture, including my family who cheered me on.

To Dolly, my daughter-in-law, who spent volumes of paper and time typing and assembling my patchwork writings into the orderly book you now hold.

To Randall, my grandson, who coached me through difficult places patiently and positively, who read and reread the manuscript and made all the business arrangements.

To Mrs. Luetta Reimer, my teacher at Fresno Pacific College, who first inspired and taught me the joy of writing.

And to my cousin and friend, Jean Janzen, in whose poetry classes I learned the love of putting words together to create a poem.

To all of you, my most sincere thanks and gratitude.

ONE

Self-portrait

I am not of delicate build, nor am I "lumbering," but rather medium and average in size.

My complexion is fair, my hair is silver, and my eyes are hazel. For reasons unknown, my eyebrows are still dark and my eyelashes have all disappeared. My nose, like my body, is medium and average, probably not the kind of a nose many people would wish to tweak. My upper lip is somewhat prominent, so much so that my brothers teased me unmercifully and called me "Big Lips." My teeth are not really attached to me, and they often spend the night in the Efferdent bath while I sleep softly in my bed. My facial expression tends to be sad, but I don't feel sad.

A self-portrait must also include my outer attire. I will seldom be seen wearing "grubbies." When I was young, I wore mostly formerly-owned clothing and shoes. Maybe that's the reason I like pretty and colorful clothes now. My most favorite colors are pink, purple, and combinations thereof. I like the gleam and sparkle of jewelry. Rings and necklaces add to a well-dressed look.

My greatest weakness, though, is shoes. When I was fifteen years old, my parents allowed me to order my first pair of black high-heeled shoes from the Army and Navy catalogue, at the price of $2.98. Never was there greater bliss than when I had those beautiful shoes on my feet! I was thrilled with the look and feel of them, so much so that I wore them to bed that night and dreamed the sweetest dreams.

Today I have shoes in many styles and colors, all with high heels.

I do not have leadership qualities and don't work well under pressure. If I can work at my own pace, I can endure long hours. I do not have an inferiority complex, yet I am timid about the unknown and unfamiliar places. I have no fear of meeting people who are on a higher intellectual and cultural level; however, I hold such people in high esteem.

In many ways, I am old-fashioned. The ways of the "old country" were instilled in me by my Russian-born Mennonite Brethren parents. I firmly believe in the "honor thy father and mother" concept. "Children, obey your parents" was a strict rule throughout my upbringing, and so it remains today. Sunday was always, and is today, a holy day, a day to rest and enjoy freedom from all the daily cares and concerns. Making good use of time and keeping busy may also be considered old-fashioned.

Old-fashioned food is a strong point with me. My entire family, down to the youngest great-grandchild, has been indoctrinated by it. I dare not, and would not, serve chicken noodle soup unless I had mixed, rolled, dried, and cut the noodles myself! Paper thin crepes (we call them Russian pancakes), *zwieback*, Easter *paska, porzelchen* (raisin fritters), *vernika*, and smoked farmer sausage are all an integral part of being old-fashioned.

As sentimental and hopelessly romantic as I am, I can spend hours poring over shelves of books and cards, especially in used bookstores. Books and cards are an obsession with me. I love sending cards and receiving them. I keep them and cherish them. I have boxes of them in my storage closet. They are beautiful and meaningful to me. Valentines, birthday, Mother's Day, anniversary, get well, and friendship, I keep them all to look at and am reminded of the love and caring they represent.

POETRY—I have a passion for it. I do not write it well, correctly, or intellectually, but I write it. In my Nothing Book, I have poems in many categories, ranging from our travel from Russia to Canada, to the terrible root cellar in my parents' house, poems about sorrow and loneliness, love and mirth, the flowers and trees, wind and snow—all have found their way first into my mind and then into my book.

I was a petulant child and extremely sensitive. Being so sensitive has brought its problems into my life. I get hurt so easily. One of my resolutions is not to tell people things that might be hurtful to them. My mother said that was being tactful. I have a tendency to be pouty if I don't get what I want. On one of our United States car trips, we stopped at a roadside food stand. I had my heart and palate set on a juicy hot dog, but was given a sweet Twinkie instead. I pouted for many miles down the road! I have pretty much overcome pouting by now and have also learned to deal with anger in more subdued ways than screaming and slamming doors.

One of the joys in my long life is having friends. I value and treasure friendships. I have worked hard to keep and maintain our friends from long ago by writing letters and visiting. I have kept contact with friends I knew when I was as young as thirteen—those are precious and few, loyal and true.

Singing is a prominent part of my life. Very early on, I had a great desire to become a singer. I sang in the house, in the woods, on the way to school, always striving for the highest notes. At age ten, I sang my first solo in a school pageant. Three years later, I was the soloist in the church choir. I continued to sing in church choirs up to the age of sixty-one. In Winnipeg, I sang in the North End Church Choir for nine years, plus the Canadian Sunday School Mission Radio Choir for seven years. I feel very privileged to have shared this music ministry with my husband, Dietrich.

Dietrich and I had a very happy home life. There was always enough love and fun to go around for all six of our beautiful and healthy children. I don't think there has been another home where so many *zwieback*, cinnamon rolls, cookies, and Russian pancakes were consumed, but I enjoyed cooking and baking for my family. In the depression years, I would often have to leave out some ingredient or other and make substitutions, but that was always the challenge for me.

I have changed over the years—and I haven't changed. I am still the way God made me, hopefully improved by His grace. The following is my greatest comfort:

*"I will be your God through all your lifetime; yes, even when your hair is white with age. I made you and I will care for you. I will carry you along and be your Savior." (*Matthew 46:6 [NIV])

TWO

My Heritage

My Grandfather Wiebe

$\mathcal{P}$eter Peter Wiebe—named for his father, Peter Wiebe—was born on September 5, 1858, in South Russia, and died on December 27, 1904.

His wife, Helena (Wiebe) Wiebe, was born on October 26, 1864 and died on April 8, 1908.

A brief description of my Grandfather Wiebe, as written by my mother, Katharina (Wiebe) Warkentin:

"My beloved father was a mild-mannered person. He gave thought before he spoke. He was a minister of the Mennonite Brethren church.

"He farmed to make a living for his family, but his interest was in creating and making things. He made a seed drill and a *Putzmuhle* (a machine that separated the chaff from the grain before it was planted). He was also a good blacksmith.

"He was very musical. When he was young, living in Michelsburg, South Russia, he was known as "Fiddle Peter." He made a fiddle for my brother Peter and a guitar for me, as well as a cymbal. He also made a pump organ of only one octave. Not being satisfied with that, he sold it and made another with two octaves, which he also sold. Finally, he made a four-octave keyboard with the half-toned black keys. He filed the metal "strings," or tone bands, by hammering old copper milk bowls and cutting them into narrow strings. The keys were made out of animal bones found in fields or pastures. The bones were first boiled (to whiten them), then cut to size and polished.

"Father would have liked me to learn how to make paper flowers, but, sadly, there was never enough money to buy things that were not absolutely necessary.

"He was a good strict father and always held morning and evening devotions with his family."

My Grandmother Wiebe

I regret that I know so little about my Grandmother Wiebe. She and Grandfather died many years before I was born.

I do know that after Grandfather's death, Grandmother, at age 44, was left with her four youngest children—my uncles Henry, Jake, Willie, and Daniel—and the farm to care for. Also living with her at that time was her older son, Peter (my uncle) and his wife, Helen. My mother, Katharina, was already married and living in her own home. Having no knowledge of how to run a farm, Grandmother Wiebe saw this as an impossible task.

Grandmother got frustrated, which led to deep depression and, tragically, despair. She saw no end to her problems, no light at the end of the tunnel, and she gave in to the thought of taking her own life by hanging.

Following Grandmother's death, Henry and Jake, who were in their mid-teens, were taken in by a family who, several years later, were instrumental in helping them emigrate to Borden, Saskatchewan.

The two younger boys, Daniel and Willie, were taken by another family and lived their lives in Russia, consequently suffering horribly during the terrible year so the Russian revolution.

My Grandmother Warkentin

I have only a vague recollection of my Grandmother Warkentin. I see her dressed in black from head to toe— this sweet little black bonnet with satin ribbons tied under her wrinkled chin was fascinating to me. She sat in a rocking chair with a child on her knee, sort of chanting, "Hoodle-lal-lal-lu-ta-tu-ta."

From what I heard about her, she was a stern, austere woman who played favorites with her daughters-in-law and was quite hard on my mother because Mother did not talk back to her.

After Grandfather Warkentin died, she spent a certain length of time living with her children—maybe three months with each child.

She had a special gold-plated cup and saucer that she drank from, and she would not allow anyone to carry or wash it. She took care of that herself. I regret not learning to know her.

My Father

Cornelius Peter Warkentin was born January 15, 1875, in Steinfeld, Russia. He married Katharina Wiebe in Michelsburg, Russia, on November 22, 1902. He died on June 22, 1957, in Clearbrook, British Columbia, and was buried in Hazelwood Cemetery in Abbotsford, British Columbia.

He was the son of Peter Warkentin, from Arkadak #6, who was born January 15, 1839, and died March 8, 1917. Peter married Maria Janzen, from Arkadak #6, who was born on February 16, 1840, and died in 1923.

In 1914, our father was drafted into the forestry service, where he served for three years.

My father had a ruddy complexion with just a touch of rust in his hair and mustache. He was of medium build and very quick and light on his feet. Mother told us that he had been quite spectacular on the dance floor when he was young.

He was physically strong and ran from place to place. He worked hard on the farm.

He loved horses and took excellent care of them. They were always groomed to perfection. He didn't have much use for cows, though. I think they were too messy for him. And perish the thought of milking them. That was for the women.

Dad was clean! The horses, the barn, the harness, everything had to be clean. On Saturdays, he would sweep the yard around the house with a broom. Clean!

My father was a hot-tempered man. If he was angry about one thing, he was violently angry at everything and everybody. We children were careful to stay out of his way during those times. I was never punished by him. I am told by my sisters that I was his favorite. Maybe that's why I could usually get what I wanted. We were always careful not to cross him.

I loved my father intensely. I knew he had a soft spot in his heart somewhere. If I would kiss the top of his head when I walked by his chair, his eyes would tear up. He loved to hear singing, and when company came, he would tell me to sing for them—even if it was the Watkins man or the Rawleigh man. My brother Neal and I sang the whole household to sleep many a night. I sang the highest possible soprano, and Neal sang a deep, rich bass, to the accompaniment of me chording on the old pump organ in our parlor.

As I am reflecting on those year, my heart is sad, and I wish I could sing another song for my dear father.

One evening when Dad and I were at home by ourselves (I was 16 at the time), he asked me whether I would like to see him dance. He wanted me to play something snappy for him. So I played and sang "Pink Elephants," and he whirled and danced on that smooth and shiny linoleum floor until he dropped! That dance was Dad's and my secret, and I was proud to share that with him.

He often told us two stories of that time. One day, all the personnel had to sign their names in a ledger and give their reason for leaving the base. One of the men put his reason for leaving as "wife had baby." The next man came along and, not taking the time to look, put a "ditto" under it, and so on down the page until there was a whole page of "dittos" under "wife had a baby." When the overseer discovered this, a lot of men were in trouble!

The other anecdote happened the time Mother went to visit Dad in the forestry. They were served tea out in the lilac arbor. My brother Neal, an infant, was in a hanging cradle, apparently without a diaper, when all of a sudden there was a little stream out of the cradle and right into Father's teacup—much to the chagrin of our impeccable father and the embarrassment of my mother!

Another brother, Peter number three, died during the time of Father's service in the forestry, shortly before my birth. Mother send word to Dad of the time of the burial, but no word came from Dad. They went ahead with the funeral, and still Dad didn't come. Then, at the cemetery, after the casket was buried, they heard the gallop of horses as Dad arrived too late to see his third son Peter before he was buried. That must have been excruciatingly painful for all concerned. Then, eight days before I was born, my grandfather died. If so may calamities should befall us these days, we would surely begin to wonder whether God still loved us.

*

Evensong

Father sat at the end of the table—
His place of honor.
Thin soft hair neatly in place,
Rusty mustache
Carefully trimmed.
He is the head of our household.

Morning, he read a Bible lesson
From a page of the daily calendar.
His small gold-rimmed spectacles
Glinting in the sunlight.
He was stern and in control,
But a light kiss on his forehead
Brought tears to his eyes.

The days were work-filled,
But the evening songs
    Were sung for him.
My unskilled fingers seeking
    For blending chords
On the ancient pump organ,
Voices blending in harmony,
Brother Neal and I sang,
    "Would you be free from
        Your burden of Sin?
    Christ has buried our transgressions
        In the deep, deep sea.
    What a wonderful Savior,
        He hideth my soul
        In the cleft of the rock."

Finally, gradually—a peaceful house,
    Fire softly crackling
    In the pot-bellied heater,
Flames visible through
The small isinglass openings.
Outside, the white moon
Causes the snow to glisten
Like a sea of diamonds
    Dancing in a wonderland
        Of unbroken distance.

The animals sheltered in the barn,
Satisfied after their evening feeding,
    Are sighing into sleep
    On their beds of
        Yellow straw.

The turbulence of the day
        Is over.
    Our songs are sung.
We walk stealthily up the stairs
So as not to waken the
        Sleeping ones,
    And silently seek our repose
    With grateful hearts
    For a happy family—
Father, mother and children—
    Tied together
    In bonds of love.

My Mother

My mother was born Katharina Wiebe on September 12, 1884, in Michelsburg, South Russia. She died on November 30, 1970. Here, in her own words, is her obituary:

"I was born on September 12, 1884, the oldest of ten children. My parents were Peter and Helena Wiebe of South Russia in Furstenland, in the Village of Michelsburg.

"In 1902, I was married to Cornelius Warkentin, in the village of Steinfeld.

"Twelve children were born to us. (Three sons, all named Peter, died.) When the situation in Russia became extremely difficult, we had the privilege of emigrating to Canada. With God's help, we were able to leave Arkadak, Russia, on August 4, 1925, and arrived in Borden, Saskatchewan, in October of 1925, after being detained in Southampton, England, for thirty days due to our two youngest daughters' skin rashes.

"We were welcomed by my brother, Peter Wiebe, and his wife. They were our hosts for sixteen days, after which we were able to rent a small house for our family.

"We experienced much love and kindness in Borden, for which I am still grateful.

"In 1941, we moved to British Columbia, where we bought a berry farm near the town of Haney after a short time in Vancouver.

"When my dear husband began to lose his eyesight, we moved to Clearbrook, B.C. Here, on June 22, 1957, my dear husband and father of our children passed away. Three of our infant sons preceded him in death. My remaining nine children mourned his going.

"I became a Christian in my teen years, was baptized and accepted as a member of the Mennonite Brethren Church in 1921. With God's help, I want to remain a faithful member.

"I have three brothers living: Peter Wiebe, and his wife Helena; Henry Wiebe, and his wife Anna, in British Columbia; and Wilhelm, and his wife, still in Russia.

"My nine children are all married, and I have 34 grandchildren and 14 great-grandchildren. In 1964, I chose to live with my oldest daughter Mary and her husband Julius Durksen. I want to stay with them until my death, but sometimes God's ways are different than our plans.

"The way He leads will be right."

Mother was soft-spoken, not easily excited or provoked, and not quick to pass judgment. On Sundays, she attended church services and was the soloist in the choir, filling the church with her beautiful, rich voice.

My mother was a sweet, mild, and meek lady. We could have a lot of fun with her. She had a difficult life with so many children to care for and so few of the necessities of life.

Mother loved to sing. Her parents were very poor and she didn't have the proper clothes or shoes for Sundays, so she sang her solos in her bare feet. She played the guitar, and she taught me and my sisters to play, too.

According to my father, he married my mother at the tender age of 17. This is what I know of her in her youth:

She had a great love for reading and a marvelous capacity to remember the people and places she read about.

She was thin with not even an outline of any unsightly

bulges underneath the heavy, dark clothing she wore—layers of skirts reaching down to her ankles, long sleeves, and high necklines of white lace at the throat, with tiny tucks and countless small buttons down to her slim-corseted waist. Her hair was dark. The thick braid tied with a ribbon fell to her waist. On her wedding day, she put her braid up in a tight knot (a *shups*) and carefully pinned a large white bow over the knot to signify that she was now a married woman.

Viewing herself in the cracked mirror, she saw a smooth skin, flawless, with no imperfections so common to youth. Hers was a composed face—full mouth and delicately chiseled nose. One earlobe was shorter than the other. Her deep-set, dark gray eyes gave her a soulful look, as though there was some great sorrow hidden in their depths.

Her beautiful, slender hands were seldom idle. They were the hands of an artist—shaping, molding, and beautifying the lives and minds of her children. Those gentle hands folded in prayer were a tribute to God, in whom she so firmly believed.

My Mother's Hands

Her gentle hands
Lying quiet now, and still,
Were tenderly suppliant
To God's will.

Her arms that once
So warmly pressed me to her breast,
Embraced me in my youth.
By their comfort I was blest.

Her hands wiped bitter tears
And applied healing balm,
While soft caressing
Soon created sweetest calm.

Still oft I long for her to tuck me in
When I am weary, or when sad.
Her hands would kindle memories,
And I could weep for solace I once had.

THE only Christmas I ever spent with my mother after I was married was in 1965. My father had passed away in 1957, and Mother was living with my sister Mary and her husband in Clearbrook, British Columbia. That visit was the inspiration for the following poem.

❀

Mother

*The last fond memories I have of my mother
Are those that we spent just loving each other.*

*Gone were the trials of younger years,
Gone were the heartaches and the tears.*

*She left her native land of birth
To live halfway across the Earth.
She taught us to cook, to knit and to mend,
And loved us all dearly right up to the end.*

*The very last Christmas I spent in her presence
Was filled with a rare and loving essence.
There were no gifts, there was no tree,
But there was great happiness inside of me.*

*I remember that night when, instead of sleep,
I looked out upon the wintry deep—
The moon and stars in their radiant splendor
Poured forth a thought that I had to ponder—
To live and to love is a God-given wonder.*

❀

THREE

My Birth

*M*arch 17, 1917 was not at all a pleasant day. Quite early in the day, the sky looked gray and foreboding, casting strange shadows over the already high snow drifts along the path leading to the street and the more uneven path leading next door to my uncle and aunt's house. The snow was now almost to the top of the wooden fence with the narrow swinging gate. The near gale wind that blew as the day wore on was sure to bring more snow by nightfall.

So, on this blustery day with the threatening storm, in the confines of my parents' home, my mother too was restless and somewhat apprehensive, for she was about to give birth to another child. She could not help but think back to the three babies that lay buried under the now thick blanket of snow and cold outside. How heartbreaking those experiences had been. Possibly only those who have gone through it could fully understand. All three of the little boys had been named Peter, for it was customary in those days to name the first-born son (or daughter) after the grandparent. In their case, both grandfathers were named Peter.

While Mother was thinking about her family, she began to slowly prepare for the birth of this new child. They had three girls by now, and one son, whom they had named Cornelius after our father.

No doubt the layette for the new baby consisted mostly of carefully washed and mangled items (done on a machine for smoothing fabrics by pressing them between rollers—this was cranked by hand and was very hard work). So with prayer and faith she got everything ready.

The wind rattled the doors and windows so that the white muslin curtains swayed. Soon it began to snow, and Mother became fearful about the oncoming night. What if the storm got so bad that Dad wouldn't be able to get out to fetch the midwife?

True to mid-March tradition, the snow and wind had their frolic, and soon it turned into a raging blizzard.

At some time during the night, Dad had to wake the younger children, wrap them in blankets, and carry them down the snow-filled path to Uncle Abe and Aunt Anna Warkentin's. He woke up the sleeping aunt and uncle and told them that by morning there would be yet another member of the family.

And so I was born in Arkadak, Russia, in Village Number Seven, five days before the Russian Revolution—born into a nation of conflict. The Russian Revolution, which caused the abdication of Czar Nicholas II on March 12, 1917, and was affected by the Duma, ultimately resulted in the establishment of the USSR. Whether or not the unrest in the country had anything to do with my temperament, I do not know. But according to my second oldest sister, Tena, who was responsible for a good part of caring for me, I was a rather willful, stubborn, rebellious, and grudge-bearing youngster; not swift to obey, but very swift to have my feelings hurt. She also was quick to add (after the above-mentioned faults) that I was very cute and most lovable when I was being good. I was accepted into the family with loving care.

Since I was born on St. Patrick's Day, I have always wished my name could have been Patricia Anne, but I've had to get along without the Patricia.

*

Annie is Born

I was born in a day of unrest and strife.
In such tragic times began a new life.
No one was safe in their home at night,
Women and children living in fright.

The years creep by—the war does not cease,
Violence and looting on the increase.
My father in service and family alone
Brings many a heartache to those left at home.

Trials and troubles, not a few,
Sickness and death of a son to live through.
They waited in agony for Father to come,
But the funeral was over when Father came home.

Eight days before me, my grandfather died.
Such sadness and sorrow, the tears scarcely dried,
The family distraught and Father away
Must have made mine a traumatic birthday!

The farmers were ordered to give up their grain.
How could they hope to ever make gain?
The best of the animals taken away,
The fear in their hearts growing stronger each day.

The family now grown in number to eight,
What will eventually be their fate?
The food so diminished, where could they turn
As around them their homes were destroyed to burn?

Then comes hope of leaving this country of hate.
Thank God! This help comes before it's too late.

The villagers gathered to form a plan,
Working together, man to man.

The women baked zwieback and toasted them brown,
Then all of the wickerware baskets came down
To be filled to the brim with food to eat
Lest some mishap on their journey they meet.

By wagon and freight train finally leaving,
On ship and ocean wave, rolling and heaving.
Soon, soon they'd be free in the land of their choice,
Where young and old in glad song would rejoice!

But, lo—in England comes a hard blow—
Sister Susan has pox so she cannot go.
Our parents stayed with her, and we set sail.
Such agony then in our hearts did prevail.

Mary and Tena, Helen and Neal,
Anne and Frank—how did we feel?
As lost and forsaken and seasick beside,
While our ship struggled on in the briny tide.

So thankful were we when our feet touched ground.
On the wind-swept depot by our uncle we were found.
An apple and candy bar placed in our hand,
Assured us we had come to the Promised Land.

The Lord and this land give us blessings indeed,
Supplies and provides for us all that we need.
Goodness and mercy He doth richly bequeath,
His everlasting arms are constant beneath!

*

FOUR

Life in Russia

We were comfortable in our house, with only a wall and Dutch door between the kitchen and the barn. The roof was straw-thatched; the walls were covered with a mixture of finely chopped straw and animal dung and applied with a mortar board until smooth. It had to dry thoroughly and then was whitewashed. The white lime was pulverized, mixed with water, and applied with a wide brush.

Some of the houses in our village were red brick with red slate roofs—the wealthier people owned those.

Our kitchen had a dirt floor. Every Saturday, after all the baking and cleaning was done, my oldest sister Mary would mix white sand and water, making a thin, runny paste, and carefully take a handful and make curlicue designs all over the black floor. It looked quite beautiful to us, unaccustomed as we were to linoleum or carpeting.

The sand was also a dust deterrent.

In one part of the kitchen, there was a trap door that led down to the cellar—the most dreaded of all places. Though I don't recall the contents of the cellar in Russia, I very vividly recall the cellars in Canada, and very often still dream about their dark and horrifying inhabitants.

❀

The Farm Cellar

"I need potatoes," my mother sighed.
I hoped it was not me she spied,
As o'er her work she bent her head.
Surely she'd call Sue or Elsie instead.

E'en though I was in the midst of song,
The call came again before too long.
Potatoes were in the cellar deep,
The most dreaded place where creatures creep.

I light the old lantern to take down with me,
Its smoky light will help me to see
The crock with the sauerkraut, the jars on the shelf,
Of rhubarb and blueberries that I picked myself.

I gather up courage and lift that trap door.
I dread that dark hole with the winter's store

Of potatoes and carrots buried in the sand,
Onions and cabbage that smell of the land.

Now down to the cellar where creatures crawl,
Where containers of home-rendered lard, large and small,
A barrel of apples that we dare not touch,
For these are doled out, lest we take too much.

I gingerly work my way down those stairs,
With lantern in hand and a heart full of prayers
That none of those creatures, however small,
Over my hands or feet will crawl.

I sing at full voice and make noises galore
And hope there's no horror in this cellar's store
As I dig for potatoes o'ergrown with roots,
While I shiver and shake in my garden boots.

When, oh, in a flash, a lizard glides near,
I grab up the lantern and cry out in fear.
I dash up those stairs and say, "Never more
Will I venture beneath that dreadful trap door!"

Our garden was always very neat. The rows of flowers and vegetables were exactly straight and in line with the next row. Some of the flowers were in raised beds, and there was also a raised pathway through the garden from which we children did not dare to stray. We also had some apple trees, and of course every garden had gooseberry bushes. The only time I could eat those terribly sour tidbits was after they turned color, got soft, and were ready to drop off the plant—so delectably sweet then.

And speaking of gardens, our neighbors, the Johann Dycks, had marvelously big cherry trees. Big, dark red cherries, probably Bings. We used to remove the pits and then fit the cherry over each one of our fingertips. After admiring them awhile, we would deliciously pop them into our mouths, one by one, and enjoy their succulent sweetness.

Harvest time was exciting, watching the threshing of the grain. No, not by machines and tractors, but on the ground, with a horse pulling a heavy log or rock around and around over the cut stalks. Then the grain and chaff were tossed by shovel into the air. The chaff would blow away and the grain would fall on the ground to be picked up and gathered into sacks, then taken to our nearest town, Arkadak, and ground into white flour.

One of the joys of autumn was the wonderful pumpkin harvest. Pumpkins large, pumpkins small, pumpkins round, and pumpkins long. Pumpkins were used for cattle feed. Big heaps of green, yellow, and orange pumpkins, what a delight they were to play with. As long as we didn't drop them, we could play dolls with them. Oh, what fun to have so many "dolls" in my make-believe family. I would choose the long pumpkins and carefully etch eyes, a nose, and mouth on one end. Then I would tie some type of rag shawl on the head, wrap it in an old baby blanket, and fantasize to my heart's delight!

The pumpkin seeds were a delicacy for us. They were washed and roasted to a delicate shade of brown, salted, and then we could eat as many as we wanted. That taste I still haven't forgotten.

Another wonderful treat for us was freshly roasted sunflower seeds. They don't taste anywhere as good now as they did to us back then. We would sit around the long wooden kitchen table and crack sunflower seeds, then make patterns on the table with the kernels. I can still visualize a huge house I formed—windows, doors, even the chimney with billowing smoke, a sidewalk with flowers beside it. When it was all done, I'd scoop handfuls of those delicious seeds into my hungry mouth!

Hog-butchering day was also exciting, from the squeal of the animal in the early morning to the mouth-watering sausage and spareribs that evening. My father was well-known for his skill of making the best sausage in our village.

*

Early Morning Sleigh Ride

The horse was happily
Trotting the trail,

We in the sleigh
Gleefully gliding on our way
To hog-butchering day,
With the snow steadily falling,
Daring us to taste
The snow-stars,
And wiping the soggy
Flakes from our faces
With red-mittened hands.
When suddenly the sleigh
Teetered and toppled.
We plunged headlong
Into the soft whiteness,
Patchwork quilt,
Heating stone,
And yellow straw.

LATER, the sugar beets were cut and cooked for syrup, which was then a substitute for sugar. The watermelon that weren't eaten in their season were ultimately cooked into syrup or stored up in the attic in the loose wheat for later consumption. The syrup was used in baking what we called *platz*. The batter was poured into huge baking pans and baked in the straw-heated oven. It tasted heavenly to us then, somewhat heavy and soggy, but sweet! In our family, it was baked on Saturday and eaten for Sunday afternoon *faspa*, a version of the English custom know as "high tea."

In those days, the saying "Children should be seen and not heard" held very true. When our parents had company, the grown-ups ate their meals in the parlor and we kids ate in the kitchen, seated on backless benches around the long table.

Saturdays were always special—cleaning and scrubbing and, if we were lucky, a bath! In summertime, the bath was in a wooden barrel that stood in the area between the house and barn. We used mother's soap made out of old grease. Fat and lye mixed in the right proportions were poured into a container, set overnight or so, and then cut into pieces, maybe the length and width of a hand. It was a far cry from Palmolive, to say the least! It was a gray hunk, but mighty potent. It must have killed a lot of germs or we probably wouldn't have survived.

Saturday was also baking day. Oh, the delicious mountains of golden brown *zwieback* that emerged from that oven. To heat the oven, we had to bring in heaping baskets of straw. It seemed that oven could consume an entire haystack for one heating! Our Saturday suppers consisted of freshly baked *zwieback*, bread, and milk. What a treat. Sometimes a bowl of cold cucumber soup made from clabber milk with garden-fresh, sliced cucumbers and a little salt and pepper, and possibly a dash of vinegar. Sound appetizing? It did then. The Sunday *faspa* tradition is still pretty well carried through, except now we serve cheese, cold cuts, jams, fruit, cakes, and cookies, and, in many homes, *zwieback*. Our Saturday suppers, even now when we are without guests, still consist of whatever I have baked, cheese and cold meats, and coffee or tea.

If Father gave us each one paper-wrapped candy when he came home from our nearest town, Arkadak, we accepted it as the norm, were absolutely thrilled, and made it last as long as possible.

On Easter Sunday morning, we had an Easter egg hunt. The eggs were usually hidden in amongst the tulip plants.

Easter

Easter is music with joyful sound,
Great Hallelujahs on earth abound,
Sunshine on lilies with fairest bloom,
Churches where people fill all the room.

Easter is resurrection from death,
Proof of deliverance, joy, and faith,
Bonnets with flowers, ribbons and laces,
Parades of people with smiling faces.

Easter is paska, warm and brown,
Sprinkles and frosting is their crown.

They stand like sentries, tall and straight,
Symbols of rising from death's dark gate.

Easter is singing, Rejoice, Rejoice!
Lift up your song, your heart, your voice.
Christ is risen from the dead,
Just as His Holy Word has said!

AT the end of the school year, which was in the month of May, the whole school would celebrate May Day. We all piled into ladder wagons, long wagons usually used for hauling hay or straw on a farm and pulled by a team of horses.

It was a joyous ride—happy children, their teacher, and their parents, singing all the way to the forest and stopping beside a beautiful river. Here we had our picnic. How good the pastry tasted that our mother had baked. It was a *platz* with a filling of sorrel leaves, which are long, narrow leaves similar to spinach but with a pleasant, sour tart taste. Sorrel grew in profusion in the gardens of that area. The leaves were chopped finely and mixed with sugar and flour, and were sometimes used as a substitute for fruit. It was also cooked into a *mouss* using milk and thickening for the base and eaten cold—a far cry from the cherry or *plumi mouss* we know today! We had those in Russia, too, in the years before the revolution.

In the summer, we made our fuel for the winter months. Animal dung and chopped straw were mixed in a big heap and spread in a large wooden frame. Then we children tramped in it with our bare feet until it became pliable and flat. Father evened it out and let it dry for several days, then cut it into squares and neatly piled it into cone-shaped stacks to dry completely. I recall that when we children would hear that "the Reds" were coming, we would hide inside those stacks.

We did not have a church building in our village, but we met in homes for Sunday school. I do not recall church services. We had a schoolhouse and were privileged to have Christian Mennonite men as teachers. I started first grade at age seven, so I learned the alphabet in Gothic script. I remember the long benches and desks we had. The swing in the schoolyard was wonderful; I felt on top of the world!

I can remember only two toys that were mine. One was a rag doll with a very small porcelain head. The other was a pull- oy, a little gray horse on a green platform with wheels. I enjoyed pulling that under chairs and over bridges devised from books or pieces of boards.

We had loads of fun playing house in our neighbor's yard. They had a tile roof, and when we found pieces and bits of that tile on the ground, we used them for our tea set. Believe me, it couldn't have seemed more real to us. We would break up pieces of bread and put them into our so-called plates and pour water in our cups. Later, when bread was so scarce, we used the sunflower shell or husk cakes that came from the sunflower oil processing plant. The oily shells were pressed together and tasted so good to our deprived palate.

I can remember only one time that Mother punished me severely. She had made a syrup of sugar and water and set it outside on a bench to get cool. I came along and, now knowing what it was, dumped the syrup out on the ground. With sugar and money so scarce, she was very angry and gave me a sharp slap on the face, out of sheer frustration I'm sure.

Then there was the time Dad had sharpened the plowshares on a plow he wanted to sell. He told us very distinctly not to play on it or go near it, so of course we had to find out what could be so dangerous about a sharp plowshare. I climbed up on the big iron seat, and when I scrambled down, I slipped and ran my ankle down the sharpened edge of that share and had a gaping, profusely bleeding wound under my ankle bone.

I was so scared that I sent brother Frank in to bring some type of bandage to stop the bleeding. He came back with tiny little scraps of ticking that Mother was using to make a pillow covering. Well, there was nothing I could do but go in and face the music. Mother happened to have some whey saved after making cottage cheese, and she soaked my foot, in it, dried it, pressed the flesh down firmly with her thumb, and wound a tight bandage of clean, white material around my ankle. That cut healed up beautifully.

The Bolsheviks

The years following my birth in 1917 grew progressively worse. Gypsies and Russians began to come into the villages asking for food. Soon they came and just took what they wanted.

Times got more and more difficult as the Bolsheviks, or "Reds," came into our villages. Things got so bad that we had only coarse black bread, some type of grits, and sunflower seed oil. If we were lucky, we had watermelon syrup which had been made in large kettles outdoors.

The Bolsheviks were very demanding. They took the best horses right out of our barn and later took bedding and anything else they fancied. We became nervous and frightened, living in constant fear, for we never knew when they would appear.

As time went on, food on our table became very scarce. There were meals that consisted of only grits or millet, with just a showing of watermelon or beet syrup poured over. The beautiful *zwieback* to which we were accustomed were gradually replaced by heavy, dark bread with husks in it. We ate raw potato peelings when we found them. It must have been heart-breaking for my parents. As long as we had sunflower oil, we dipped the bread in it with a little salt, which made it more palatable.

By 1924, we were hungry. There just wasn't much food available. The government took almost all the grain the farmers could produce.

About that time, we received CARE packages from Canada sent by the Mennonite Central Committee, a relief organization that sends help wherever it is needed and which is still functioning strongly today.

FIVE

Leaving Russia

*F*inally, in 1925, the people in our village got word that we could leave for Canada. Mother's brother, Peter Wiebe, lived in Borden, Saskatchewan, and would take us in when we arrived. The Canadian Pacific Railroad paid passage for us with the stipulation that we pay them back after we got established in Canada.

The one thing I had overheard about Canada was that it had steep, high mountains, and we would have to drive straight up to the top and come straight down the other side. That seemed terribly frightening to me—maybe that's why I still have a fear and dread of driving in the mountains.

What an emotional time that must have been for my parents, to uproot their entire home and all their belongings. But they knew they could not survive in Russia.

Then began the hustle and bustle of preparation—things to sell and give away, clothes for all eight children, what to take and what to leave behind. The last few days, Mother baked *zwieback*. I don' know where or how they managed to get white flour. The *zwieback* were cut into bite-sized pieces and then browned in the oven. They were packed into big baskets or wicker trunks for the journey, easily accessible for hungry children when nothing else was available.

We had to have medical examinations and passport pictures. For my picture, I wore a bright blue dress with white polka dots and a white collar that Mother had crocheted. My hair was slicked back with two of the scrawniest, silky pigtails you ever saw. But we were going to Canada!

Finally, in August, when all was said and done, we were driven to the train depot in Arkadak, where we were assigned a cattle car of a freight train and given Canadian Pacific Railroad pins, which we wore all the way to Borden, Saskatchewan. This particular boxcar was filthy with cow dung, so some of our party had to shovel, scrape, and scrub before we could be boarded. It took several days of waiting in the train before we were able to leave.

Unfortunately my recall of the three days it took us to get to Moscow is rather vague. I do have a memory of eating hot boiled potatoes with the skins on and, of course, roasted *zwieback*. It also seemed to me that the car was very crowded and uncomfortable, and that the children were constantly told to be quiet.

From Moscow, we proceeded to Riga. On the Latvian

border stood a huge, red iron gate. After the train passed through the archway, it came to a sudden stop. Everyone was allowed to disembark. We were out of Russia. We were free!

What rejoicing and celebrating there was. People were hugging and crying and laughing all at the same time. When the crowd settled down somewhat, everyone grouped together and gave prayers of thanksgiving, after which we all sang, with great fervor, that majestic old hymn, "Now Thank We All Our God."

Now thank we all our God
With hearts and hands and voices.
Who wondrous things hath done,
In whom this world rejoices.

Who from our mothers' arms
Hath blessed us on our way
With countless gifts of love
And still is our today.

We were finally free from the terrorism of the Russian government and were now heading for an unknown country with unknown customs and language. But we were free, going to a land of plenty. What jubilation and thanksgiving filled our hearts! Singing that hymn still fills me with awe and tender emotion. Listening to the beautiful voices of those men and women was overwhelming. Up to that hour, those men had been fearful of being taken out of the train and shipped to Siberia. Some men were actually taken from the train before Latvia, never to be heard from again. Tearful women were clinging to their husbands, and children were hanging onto their mothers' clothing.

After arriving in Riga, we were escorted to a large building, possibly a barracks, where we stayed only a short time, maybe a day and night. The food they gave us tasted strange and unfamiliar.

From Riga, we boarded the ship *Baltara* and headed for Southampton, England. The dining room, which was deep in the bowels of the ship, did not hold much interest for us because, one by one, we were smitten by seasickness.

After seven days, we reached Southampton, England, on August 24, 1925. Here we had medical examinations and steam baths. Our clothes were fumigated and our heads shaved, all except Mary and Tena. I remember that my plaid dress had those nasty little lice hidden in the seams. Those varmints did not make it out of that fumigation!

My two younger sisters, Susan, two, and Elsie, ten months, had a rash on their skin. The medical examiner said it was contagious and refused to let them go on to Canada. This was a real crisis! They had to be in quarantine for thirty days. Our parents had to make an extremely difficult decision—should Mother stay behind with the babies and let Dad go with the rest of us? Not knowing a word of English, Mother did not want to stay alone, so Dad stayed with her and the girls. That meant that Mary, the oldest at age nineteen, would be in charge of Tena, Helen, Neal, Anne, and Frank, who was six years old.

We were in Southampton for three days, and then embarked on the ship *Melita*, which was a Canadian Pacific passenger line. I do not remember any of the trauma and terror of leaving our parents behind.

I do, however, remember the room on that ship, next to the engine room, swaying and bobbing from side to side. We all lay in our bunks just wanting to die. The fumes of the oil and grease from the engines were so terrible to our already sick stomachs.

The food they brought us was indescribably awful. Coffee with cream and sugar, celery that tasted like coal oil, oranges…oh, what a dreadful smell. I couldn't eat a bite of anything.

After five days, some authorities looked in on us and removed us from that room. We had been put in there by mistake! We all had to be carried out, for we were too weak to walk. After nine days on the heaving ocean, we arrived in Quebec, Canada, at the mouth of the St. Lawrence River. From there we were put on a Canadian Pacific Railroad train bound for Borden, Saskatchewan. I was sick again, just like on the ship, and wondered if I would ever feel good and be able to run and play and eat again.

So, after a long and discouraging journey in railroad boxcars and heaving ships on a stormy ocean, we were relieved to set food on the dry, solid ground of Borden.

SIX

Canada

Borden, Saskatchewan

*O*n September 8 1925, the jolting train came to a stop. We had reached our final destination. Our uncle, Peter Wiebe, was to meet us at the train station. As we stood forlornly on that bleak depot platform and waited for him to come claim us, we watched as other people were met. One by one, everyone left, until only the six weary, travel-worn strangers were left standing on that lonely platform.

Finally, a woman took pity on us and, with much gesturing, led sister Mary to a telephone and helped put a call through to Uncle Peter, who was supposed to meet us there. Somehow he had not received the letter my mother had sent him from England as to the time of our arrival.

We were taken into a little hotel then and given something to eat by the same lady—probably the station agent's wife, but I'm not sure. She served us bran muffins, which we liked.

After what seemed a very long time, a Mr. Wall arrived in a touring car. Uncle Peter had sent him. We were overjoyed when he gave us each a candy bar and a big, beautiful red apple...all our own! Never has there been such joy! Oh, that tasted wondrously delicious—my first taste of chocolate. My eyes are brimming with tears as I recall that moment. We saved the wrapper of that chocolate bar; it was so precious to us.

We were warmly welcomed by Uncle Peter and Aunt Helen Wiebe, and their ten children. Their children were lined up in front of the kitchen range according to age. That image is still clear in my mind today. They could not keep all of us, so Uncle Henry and Aunt Anna Wiebe came and took me and my sister Helen, who was four years older than me. We stayed with them for one month.

In 1926, when our family was all back together, we lived in a tiny, two-room house in Great Deer, Saskatchewan, in the Borden area. There were not beds for all of us. My bed consisted of chairs pushed up against the wall in the kitchen—the backs of the chairs facing into the room—with blankets and a pillow for bedding. First thing in the morning, Mother made a fire in the kitchen stove, which woke me, and I had an overwhelming sense of love and security just because Mother was there. What a tremendous role and influence a mother has on the lives of her children, and what a blessing to have a godly Christian mother!

My older sisters soon got work in neighbors' homes, and we younger children were sent to school. We soon discovered that if we were to survive, we had to learn to speak English. There were many embarrassing moments, and the other children thoroughly enjoyed our frustration.

Zeneta, Saskatchewan

It wasn't long before our family was on the move again. With the depression years almost upon us, it was difficult for our father to eke out a living for a large family. There was a farm in Zeneta, Saskatchewan, that seemed to hold out some hope for a better future, or was it just the old saying, "Far pastures look greener"? In any case, the decision was made to move to Zeneta by train.

Although we did not have many earthly possessions, moving always causes a great upheaval with much hustle and bustle. I'm sure we children were not much help in the preparation for this move.

We were chilled by the time we arrived at the small train depot in Borden. We crowded around the pot-bellied heater trying to warm our bodies, and listened in awe to the clickety-clack of the telegraph machine in the corner.

The platform outside was desolately forsaken and deserted. The fierce north wind drove icy particles of snow across the bare wood and into our anxious faces every time we came out of the building to watch for the train.

The bleak landscape of the Canadian prairie seemed God-forsaken in its endless blanket of snow.

Finally, the smoking monster became visible and soon arrived with a great blow of its shrieking whistle, which echoed in the untamed wilderness.

There was a great scramble then to get on board with all the bundles and belongings we carried with us. We were hoisted, pulled, and pushed. Our parents wound up in the procession with the smaller children. How my heartaches even now for the burden and pain my parents had to endure in those difficult years.

The train seats were upholstered in dark green plush, which looked warm and inviting to our chilled-to-the-bone bodies.

After the doors were closed and the train gathered speed, we smelled the coal gas from the engines. It permeated everything, and very soon we began to feel nauseous. The bread and butter sandwiches that Mother had brought tasted of it, and even the milk we brought absorbed the taste and smell.

Sleep was almost impossible, with the bumps, lurches, and screeching of the brakes on the frozen rails. As the night wore on, I became aware of another problem—my feet hurt! I was wearing a pair of hand-me-down shoes with a mid-heel that were much too large for me, so I had stuffed the toes generously with newspaper until they stayed on my ten-year-old feet. After having worn them in the extreme cold all day, my toes began to hurt in the warmth of the train. I was too proud to take the shoes off or admit my pain, so I suffered in silence. Consequently, at age 73, I have acquired a good sized bunion on my right foot, which I believe is a result of wearing ill-fitting shoes in my growing years.

The two-story house that was to be our home on that lonely farm in Zeneta looked anything but inviting and friendly. The bare windows stared blankly, as if hiding a lifetime of dark secrets. The wood exterior had long since faded, not a vestige of paint on the weather-beaten boards remained, giving them the appearance of aged pewter.

The wooden board sidewalk leading to the small, rickety porch was hazardous with pieces broken and missing.

The kitchen was a lean-to—an afterthought added to the house. This made it the coldest room of all (not that *any* of the rooms were ever warm!) except in the few summer months when it would be intolerably hot.

In the winter months, when we wiped the kitchen table with a wet cloth, it immediately turned into a frozen glaze, and we could send plates gliding from one end to the other like skaters on ice. The oatmeal didn't stay hot very long in that freezing atmosphere.

The living room was square, with a staircase leading up on one side. The pot-bellied heater in the middle of the room had to be fed continuously to keep both downstairs and upstairs bedrooms warm.

Several of us children took tumbles down these steep stairs. One of the younger sisters tried to carry baby Allan down one day. They both landed in a pitiful heap at the bottom, with Allan's head hitting hard against a chest of drawers. Thankfully there were no severe or lasting injuries.

When we first moved into the house, we found the name "Wittenberg" written on the wall at the top of the stairs. We often wondered who might have belonged to that name. Much later in our sojourn, we learned to know those Wittenbergs, and they became fine and loyal friends. Jack and his wife Mary live in Richmond, British Columbia, and Henry and Jean live in Clearbrook.

It was in their house that I experienced baking my first cake. Mother and Dad were away for the afternoon, and I wanted to do something nice as a surprise for them when they came home. I began by getting paper and kindling to build a fire in the kitchen range, a big, black hulk with a warming oven on top and a reservoir for water on the end away from the firebox.

After finding a recipe for a plain white cake, I assembled the ingredients and laboriously mixed, added, and stirred (no electric mixers then). I poured the batter into a far-too-large pan and put it into the oven to bake. The cake looked fine, although somewhat anemic. I just couldn't wait to sample it. But, alas and alack, I had forgotten to put in the sugar. Oh, what a disappointed girl I was.

THE one-rooom school we attended was several miles away, so we had to drive. Our oldest brother Neal drove us in the one-horse open sleigh. Mother usually had some heated bricks or rocks that we put in the sleigh, along with a thick layer of clean straw. With Mother's home-made blankets, we managed to stay relatively warm. Although we encountered many an ice blizzard so fierce that we could barely see the snow-filled road, our trusty brown "Prince" always found his way home with all of us intact. Wonder of wonders!

I was involved in the school play that Christmas. I don't recall much of what took place that evening, except that while I was changing my costume behind the make-shift curtain, one of the boys accidentally lifted a corner of the curtain. I screamed. I'm sure everybody thought I was being murdered, but I was just so frightened.

After the play, Santa came and distributed the gifts from under the tree. To my utter delight and totally un-expected, I received three presents. They were the first wrapped gifts I had ever received. I almost believed in San-ta Claus! A box of three embroidered linen handkerchiefs, a long string of beautiful blue genuine glass beads, and a little box of fancy notepaper. The gifts were from a secret admirer or Santa, I don't know which, but I was totally overwhelmed and happy.

Our outdoor sport that winter was trying to skate on our frozen pond. We spent hours clearing the snow from a large area and then had fun sliding and slipping along. The surface was never completely smooth. It had ruffles and ridges, but we took turns wearing the one pair of skates we had. Many a bruise and bump were suffered as a result of that skating experience.

In the summer, that pond was murky and slimy and infested with water snakes and jumbo mosquitoes that were torture to us.

The vegetable garden that Mother and Dad planted was in perfectly straight rows, thanks to Dad, and yielded a variety of crisp, fresh, and succulent produce. Many a carrot and radish was pulled out of the ground and eaten by us children long before they were matured. We just couldn't wait! Poppies and cosmos grew in a profusion of color all over the garden. Dad would allow that, but he was death on weeds.

When winter came and the snow covered the frozen garden, nothing remained except the poppy heads on their long stems protruding through the snow. We picked those pods and ate the seeds. It was a treat for us. At that time we had no knowledge of what was contained in those tiny, black seeds. We only knew they tasted good.

One Sunday afternoon, my older sister Helen and I were left at home by ourselves. We had no ration, TV, or books for entertainment, so we tried to think of something fun to do. We raided the attic and found some old clothes. We put them on and we looked terrible, like the worst slum children. We decided that maybe we could look like clowns, but we needed powder. We raided the pantry for white flour that would do nicely and painted our cheeks with red crepe paper. Now we really looked like clowns.

We hardly had a chance to admire each other when things suddenly came to a screeching halt, for we saw a car approaching our long driveway. That could only mean Sunday visitors. Woe unto us ragged urchins, what shall we do?

We flew to the wash basin in the kitchen, washed our faces with cold water, which made the flour turn into pink paste but did not faze the red color on cheeks, lips, or noses. What a dilemma. We had to go as we were to face the people in the car. Fortunately they were strangers asking for directions. After they left, Helen and I went into fits of laughter to the point of hysteria. The red on our faces had to be scrubbed off with Mother's homemade soap and Dutch cleanser. Such are the antics of the young.

WE had to haul our drinking water from our neighbor's well because the water in our well tasted bitter. This was fairly routine with Dad and the boys. One bitterly cold winter day, however, it turned out to be a near tragedy.

For some reason, Helen was to drive the team of horses with the water barrels in the sleigh. The snow was deep and packed hard. For the most part, she drove over the top of the snow. When Helen didn't return on schedule, we got anxious at home. We waited and worried. Finally, we saw Helen come stumbling home across the snow, half frozen and minus the horses and sleigh. Shaking and crying, she told us that the horses had fallen through the snow and had gotten tangled in a wire fence. In spite of their pouncing and pulling, they could not free themselves from the wire and the deep snowdrift. It was a dreadful scene, but Dad sprang into action. He grabbed a pair of wire cutters and made his way to the stranded team where he managed to free the poor injured horses and brought them all home to the shelter of the warm barn.

Dad loved his horses and always took excellent care of them. He faithfully treated their injuries with the famous cure-all, Watkins carbolic salve. With plenty of TLC and extra measures of good oats, the two horses survived their terrible ordeal.

While Dad took care of his team, our dear mother soothed Helen's shattered nerves and, no doubt, gave her some homemade chicken noodle soup, a cure-all in every Mennonite or Jewish family.

FOR some unknown reason, I dream I am back in the Zeneta house. In my dream, there is an extra large bedroom upstairs with three beds that are always ready to sleep in. The sheets and pillows are white, but never fresh or clean. I always feel secure there. Who can interpret such a recurring dream?

I was ten years old (going on sixteen, I guess) when my fantasies and longings seemed to have no end. I was lonesome in spite of a house full of siblings and my parents. I was looking and wishing for something beautiful, but I didn't rightly know what. Life was like a hard scrabble and colorless.

I longed for pretty clothes, bright and colorful ones. My ideas must have come straight out of the T. Eaton's mail order catalogue, for there certainly weren't any fashion models in that barren plain to catch my fancy. I spent endless hours poring over the pages of that wish book. The lacy, filmy unmentionables for ladies (we wore mother-sewn flour sack undies), the beautiful red dresses with patent leather belts (I can always settle for red!)—and shoes. I only looked at shoes with high heels. I was enchanted by the dainty look of the catalogue ladies' feet and ankles wearing those pretty shoes.

My clothes were "formerly owned," and the dresses were often ill-fitting. One of my dresses at that time was a light green wool serge that Mother made over for me. There was not enough material to make long sleeves, so she used dark green for the lower half of the sleeve. Why do I remember that particular dress so vividly, nearly seventy years later? Two reasons: I didn't like green, and it made my skin itch.

With this uncomfortable two-toned dress, I had to wear black wool stockings that my sweet mother had knit by hand—and I hated them. They were so ugly and made my legs look so fat. Beside that, they made me itch even more than the dress. Hard times indeed for a young girl with dreams in her head.

I also chose a coat on the catalogue's color page. A beautiful magenta color, trimmed with gray fur. In my fantasy, it was already mine. Fifty-five years later, I had an outfit that color with a silver fox fur.

Whenever possible, I would escape the reality of the house to walk in a wooded area a short distance away, where I pretended I was a lovely lady dressed in the magenta coat and smart, high-heeled shoes, walking on a smooth, concrete sidewalk in a far off city. I was totally unaware of the rough path and the brambly bushes that caught at my clothes and hair, so intense was my childish longing and desire.

Some years later, in 1933, one of my dreams was fulfilled when my father allowed me to order a pair of high-heeled T-strap shoes out of the Army and Navy mail order catalogue. Even as I write this, I feel the surge of excitement that I felt when those black shoes were first put on my feet. It was total joy! I was so thrilled with the look and feel of them that I kept them on all night and had the sweetest dreams.

Many years and many smooth sidewalks later, in my old age when I should know better, I still like to wear high heels, as well as bright, colorful clothing.

I look back now and, deep inside, can recall the feelings I had in the long ago. I am a hopeless romantic and a sentimentalist to this very day.

"Why do you worry about clothes? See how the lilies of the field grow. They do not labor or spin. Yet I tell you that not even Solomon in all his splendor was dressed like one of these." (Matthew 6:28)

WE did not have church services on a regular basis in that community, nor did we have a church building. But whenever possible, we would gather in different homes and have services led by one of the laymen.

One such service was held in our home. This was led by a minister of the Seventh-Day Adventist Church who had come by special invitation to minister to the Mennonite group.

Mr. Neufeld's text that night was Daniel, chapter 5, which begins with King Belshazzar's feast. It was while the King was drinking, feasting, and merry-making, praising the gods of gold, silver, brass, iron, wood, and stone, that he suddenly saw a hand-writing on the wall in a language that he did not know. The King was greatly troubled and so afraid "that the joints of his loins were loosed, and his knees smote one against another."

The interpretation of verse 27 is, "Thou are weighed in the balance and art found wanting." This hit home. In my heart and mind, I was the one being weighed, and in the sight of God, I was found wanting. I felt a great need in my soul and began to weep.

At the close of the sermon, the preacher asked whether there was anyone who wanted to accept the gift of salvation. I wanted that very much, but immediately a struggle began in my mind. What would happen? What would everybody think of me if I put up my hand? I wept and prayed and fought within. Almost without my own effort, my hand went up! I felt the most wonderful peace and love flood my whole being, and immediately I was surrounded by white angels with golden wings. I felt so free and unburdened. I could have joined those angels and gone right to heaven with them. Such joy and happiness I had never before felt. My sins were forgiven, and I belonged to Jesus.

That night I dreamed I saw two paths before me. One was the broad way, which led to destruction ("…and many there be which go in thereat." Matthew 7:13). The other was the narrow way ("Because strait is the gate, and narrow is the way, which leadeth unto life, and few there be that find it." Matthew 7:14).

When I awoke from this dream, I knew I had chosen the narrow way, and again I was overcome with joy.

I went downstairs in the middle of the night and told my parents that I had accepted Jesus as my Savior. They were happy for me, and Mother and I knelt on that icy cold floor and thanked God for accepting me as His child.

At the age of eleven, I accepted Christ as my own personal Savior, and two years later was baptized in the river not far from our home in Margaret, Manitoba. I was received as a member in the Mennonite Brethren church.

I know that if God can reach into the very remote part of Saskatchewan to reach one young girl, He can reach everyone anywhere with His gift of salvation, full and free.

SEVEN

Teen Years

$\mathcal{I}$ have memories of how things were in our home in Margaret, Manitoba, when I was growing up as a teen in the early 1930s. When there was no work outside and Mother had time to do some fun things, she would teach us girls about sewing and embroidery.

Morning came gloriously. Sunshine streamed through the east window, the only one in the upstairs bedroom that my two younger sisters, Susan and Elsie, shared with me. Birds sang happily and noisily in the old, lone maple tree growing beside our long, narrow driveway. With the exception of a low acacia hedge across the little ravine that ran halfway around our house, there were no other shrubs or trees nearby.

Walking down the dark, unlit stairway of the house was always done at great bodily risk and was a frightening challenge. You could encounter anything from boy's boots, overshoes, winter caps and mittens, books, laundry and other items that had been on their way upstairs but never got there, to little gray mice scampering over, under, and in the flour sacks that were stored under the sloping room. (Mice were, and still are, the terror of my life!)

My Room Upstairs

The stairs are dark and steep,
And as I climb, I weep,
For there is nothing lovely at the top.

The floor once painted is now slivered.
How often have I stood and shivered?
So little heat escapes the one black stovepipe.

The metal bedstead, chipped and rusty,
The sagging mattress, lumpy, dusty,
No look of comfort there, or beauty.

The one small window frosted over,
I hurriedly seek the bed to cover
Over my head, till I breathe warm.

When sleep comes creeping at long last,
I dream my dreams and I am blest.

Gone is stark reality.

The bed has changed to comfort sweet,
The entire room is warm and neat,
The window clear of frost.

But when I wake to sound again,
I see the frost on the window pane
And feel the slivers in my feet.

I run downstairs and am embraced
By family who together faced
And coped with winter until spring
Made new creation of everything.

AFTER breakfast was over, the chores were done, like wash-ing dishes in enamel, oblong bowls, one to wash in and one to rinse (no liquid Ivory in those days—just water as hot as the hands could tolerate).

The kitchen floor was made of uneven pine boards that we scrubbed every Saturday on hands and knees. It was a light sand color when clean, but by the end of the week it was almost black again. Many beautiful dreams were dreamed by me as I labored on that floor—dreams of future floors with bright, shiny linoleum like we saw in the T. Eaton's catalogue.

Mother had flour sacks on hand most of the time. These had to be scrubbed on the washboard until most of the print was off, then bleached and boiled until they were snowy white. Out of these sacks we could make a variety of lovely things, like bib aprons, embroidered tea towels carefully hemmed, embroidered, and edged with crochet all around, tablecloths and napkins, bed sheets and slips and underwear.

Mother's favorite place to sit was beside the west window in the kitchen. There she would knit, mend, or embroider while we sat at her knee, watching and learning how to cast on stitches, then laboriously trying to knit them onto the other needle. I was so proud when I finished my first block of green and lavender, which I used for a dresser scarf in our upstairs bedroom.

On a good day, Mother would read us stories out of the German weekly *Mennonitische Rundschau*, which we enjoyed immensely. We could hardly wait for the next installment to arrive. The one story I recall was titled "Kerlchen."

Harvest time in Margaret, Manitoba, was hot and dry with the wheat and barley fields shimmering golden in the glorious sun, the oat crop white and ready to be cut. During harvest, there was no sleeping in for any member of the family. Mother and Dad were the first ones at work, killing and plucking chickens for the noon meal, stirring up starter for the bread to be baked that day. Breakfast for all of us, too!

The horses had to be fed, the hogs were squealing and grunting for their food, and the cows needed to be milked—work for everybody.

One morning Dad wanted to start cutting the barley and expected my brothers, Neal and Frank, and me to follow the binder and shock the sheaves as they came off the conveyer belt. Four horses were hitched to the binder, and Dad guided them so the grain would be cut in very straight rows. The machine cut and tied the grain into bundles that were about as big around as our teenaged arms could reach. We picked up the bundles by the twine and set them grain-side up—the first two slightly leaning into each other, the next two on the side for support, and so on until there were eight or ten sheaves in the shock. These also had to be set in straight rows.

This was hard work for us. Dad always encouraged us, and we really tried our best. Barley, as well as some wheat, has a long, harsh beard to protect the grain kernels. These beards would break apart and creep into our clothes, under our collars, into sleeves, socks, shoes, even the mouth. They were most irritating and scratchy. Add to that the burning sun and volumes of dust and you have a very uncomfortable situation.

The stubble was just tall enough to pierce our legs, so that after a day of this we had streamlets of blood flowing down our legs.

When noon rolled around, we were only too happy

when Dad called "whoa" to the horses, for that meant a hot dinner at home after a long, cool drink of water at the windmill-driven pump. After dinner, we had an hour to relax while Dad took a nap before returning to work.

By four o'clock, we began to watch for Mother to bring us a sandwich, sometimes of sliced onions and salt or leftover meat from dinner, and always a piece of cake or a cookie with hot coffee. Then two more hours of work.

After the evening meal of friend potatoes, boiled eggs, and marshmallow-soft slices of homemade bread, it was time to get cleaned up. Oh, how the broken skin on our legs burned when we washed them with homemade soap. But there wasn't a chance of infection. Mother's loving hands applied the Watkins medicated ointment.

Finally came bed and blissful, healing sleep.

In the summer the kitchen cook stove was moved into the granary so the kitchen would stay cool. We would pull the dark green window shades before the heat of the day, which gave the room a restful and comfortable feel.

In the summer, our breakfast was usually bread, *grüben schmaltz,* and coffee brewed out of oven-roasted barley that was then ground in the coffee mill and steeped in boiling water.

The winter season breakfasts were more hearty and delicious—potatoes fried in lard with an egg or two stirred in, or delectable *grüben* with thick slices of homemade bread. But mostly it was hot oatmeal.

During this time span there were usually eight or nine seated around the long kitchen table. The younger ones sat on a bench along the wall behind the table, and Dad on the west end with Mother on the side. Then my place, with Frank and Neal on the same side.

Before we could begin eating, Dad would read from a daily devotion calendar (in German), and one of the younger children said the table grace:

Vater, segne diese speise
Uns zur draft, und Dir zum Preise
(Father, bless this food
to our strength, and to your praise.)

A PHOTO of Susan, Elsie and Allan standing in the shade of the one and only tree along our narrow lane evokes in me memories like a string of precious pearls long hidden from sight. We called it "the lonely maple." Somehow it brings the past into such clear focus that I relate to it with deep emotion, for that farm was indeed a lonely place out on the prairies of Margaret, Manitoba.

Beyond the tree, the vast landscape lay in open reaches. If the pale blue sky had come any nearer to Earth, it would surely have crushed the prairie flatter than it already was. Mornings were clear and transparent, but in the gloaming, the land seemed to be floating in a sea of purple haze.

The picture shows nothing beyond the three children and the maple tree, but, oh, there was much, much more.

On Spring's fresh and bright mornings, a meadowlark sang, perched on the fence, no doubt awaiting its mate. At our feet, thrusting through the turfs of damp grass and the thin, silver crust of ice like filigreed lace, the crocus poked up their fuzzy purple heads, sparkling with sunshine and waiting to go dancing with the wind.

Then, in June, the countryside was enlivened with an incense-like fragrance from thousands of wild roses nestled in the grass along the path where we walked.

Crossing Bob King's Yard

We walked west on the well-trodden path along the barbed-wire fence to where Bob King's property began. Here I usually had to close the book of whatever enchanting story I was reading, because the field was either bumpy and rough or freshly plowed and harrowed and extremely dusty.

Turning south, we followed the winding footpath that led along the upper edge of the deep ravine, then abruptly turned down to the bottom where the welcome quiet and shade of the trees grew along the bashful stream, and the blue-green dragonflies darted in and out of the patchy sunlight.

The path continued along the bottom and eventually up into Bob King's yard. After crossing the yard, the path dipped down and we had to climb over some big boulders, traverse a bubbling brook, and ascend a steep hill. At the top, just across the narrow road, stood the Pinkham School. In this one-room schoolhouse, we spent five days a week in pursuit of our education.

To merely mention crossing Bob King's yard would not be adequate, for it was littered with an assembly of broken-down and rusty farm implements and old lumber and a barn that had been painted red in years past with doors askew on their rusty hinges.

The house that this crusty old bachelor lived in was also in need of paint and repair. It was dark and dreary, but fascinating, too. He had an old Victrola (with the horn) and many old records that he played for us. We did not have a phonograph at home, so we were delighted by this music box. That is where I first heard songs like "That Silver-haired Daddy of Mine," "Home on the Range," "I Was Taking Nellie Home," and many others.

There was also a pump organ that especially intrigued me. He played it for us and I sang along. I had been plaguing my parents for an organ or piano, but little did I dream that that old organ would be mine someday. Miracle of miracles, Dad bought it for me some years later. I still feel the wonderful excitement and thrill of the moment that organ came into our living room. I spent hour after hour playing it and singing. I forgot my household chores and duties and all other things, so enthralled was I in making music.

My brother Neal and I spent every evening singing to

my chording. I did not read music, so I played by ear. Father loved our music-making, and many a night we sang him and all the family to sleep. He never regretted spending the $25 he paid for that instrument. It was a wonderful fulfillment and joy to me. In a future time, it would be the music of this organ that would accompany my walk to the marriage altar, and my husband Dietrich and I would spend many hours singing with Neal and Frank, always at the organ.

THE books on the library shelves became my close friends and companions. *Anne of the Green Gables, A Girl of the Limberlost, David Copperfield,* and *Black Beauty* are stories I still recall with fondness and nostalgia.

Miss Laura Fleming was the sweet, kind, and gentle teacher who allowed me to play "Stand Up, Stand Up for Jesus" on the organ, even though I played only the melody with one finger. It was such a thrill for me.

Miss Doris Gorby was the pretty young teacher who gave me one of her castoff dresses. It was navy blue with a design of a cluster of big red roses.

Then there was Miss Baskerville, the stern spinster. She was not well-liked. The boys showed their disapproval one day by putting gravel in the gas tank of her green car, causing grievous inconvenience to all concerned.

What about the gray and blue speckled enamel lunch buckets we carried to and from school every day? Did I ever carry one, or was my nose and attention always in the pages of yet another book?

The bucket was rectangular in shape and had a top that we usually filled with coffee. Not coffee like we know it today, which you buy in a colorful can and pour into a Mr. Coffee! No, this coffee's base was roasted barley, ground in the coffee mill and poured in a pot with boiling water where it was allowed to "set" for awhile on the back of the stove until it was the color of coffee.

A considerable amount of this home brew sloshed over in the carrying of the lunch bucket and, sadly, seeped down onto our lard or syrup sandwiches, which were not wrapped. Needless to say, lunch frequently tasted less than delectable.

On one of sister Tena's visits home, she made us wonderfully surprising sandwiches the like of which we had never tasted. Salmon sandwiches! We thought surely we had gone to fish heaven. How proudly we ate our lunch on that memorable day and wished we could eat something so marvelously delicious again.

School hours were from nine to four. On our walk back, we began looking toward home. We could see it right after we came up out of the ravine—the windmill, the barn, and the gray, weather-beaten house. It was so sun bleached and rain soaked that, in the right light, it had a satin silvery sheen. It had been battered and beaten by many a Canadian storm, but had withstood every battle of the season.

But when we saw our mother in the garden, wearing her snowy white kerchief, our hearts and spirits were lifted high above all the cares and hurts we might have sustained during the school day, for Mother was a healer and comforter. What a wonderful feeling of security when Mother was nearby! I long for that feeling even now.

EIGHT

Winnipeg

In 1934 I left my parents' home and went to Winnipeg, where I found work. Coming from the country to the city at age 17 was a dream fulfilled in my life. My sister Helen was living and working in Winnipeg at this time, and when it came time for me to seek employment, she helped me to get used to city ways—how to get around by streetcar and how to find my way around town. On our days off, we would shop in downtown Winnipeg and sometimes go to be with Dietrich and other friends. During those two years, I worked as a live-in cook doing general housework and baby-sitting. I acquired a work ethic and learned many things that would be of great value to me throughout my life.

It would be two years before I would return home, two years of difficult, hard work, but also a time of the Lord's leading that would change my life. I had met Dietrich! Let me tell you a little about him.

Dietrich

Dietrich was born in the frozen steppes of Siberia and lived in Russia until he was twelve years old, so there were a number of things he could recall from life in his village, which was about forty kilometers from Slavgorod, Siberia.

Here, early winters were so cold and snowy that the snow banks were level with the eaves of the houses. Sleds were pulled to the top of the roof, and the ride down was exciting for the Friesen boys.

Dietrich began school in the village at age seven, walking less than a mile to the small school. Though he had little to do with the Russian peasants, at school he had to learn the Russian language. Sports at the school consisted of dodge ball games and rolling hoops, but music was what drew him. Dietrich's love of music and his skill at conducting became first evident in this little school when his teacher called on him unexpectedly, thrust a baton into his hand, and ordered him to conduct his classmates in a favorite school song. This he managed to do quite naturally, much to his own astonishment and his teacher's satisfaction.

His home in the village was typical, with shed and a barn attached to the house. There were about twenty families in the village, which also had a Mennonite Brethren church. The village was made up mostly of Mennonite Brethren families, many of whom were Friesen relatives. About thirty or so persons attended the church. These small churches in the villages occasionally got together for songfests.

Dietrich's village had only been developed since 1905 and did not have many stores. A mill was located several miles away, but most provisions had to be gotten from Slavgorod. This trip was made only two or three times a month when something special was needed. Dietrich's brother once brought apples from the city. They hadn't had any for years, and he was disappointed that his share was only a "small chunk."

The Russian revolution was felt rather indirectly in this remote village. Soldiers did not come into the village, but times were hard. All who could afford it, and some extra, left the village to look for a better life. This included many Friesen relatives. Dietrich's mother and older brothers (only three brothers were still living at this time) decided to emigrate to Canada in 1926.

Many families from the village, including some Friesen uncles, traveled by boxcar to Moscow. They left in the autumn just as it was getting cold. The accommodations in the boxcar were not first class—everyone slept on straw on the floor like cattle. The one bright spot of the trip was the huge wicker basket of *zwieback* that Dietrich's mother brought along. After arriving in Moscow and obtaining their passports, the train moved on to the Baltic Sea. They remained in the boxcar "hotel" until a ship was ready to sail for England.

The trip to England took only a few days, and Dietrich did not remember being very sick. However, people around him did. On this leg of the trip, Dietrich was given his first orange, but no instructions about how to eat it. He was surprised by a squirt in the eye as he picked at the peeling, but after it was peeled he enjoyed it immensely.

In England, the family was allowed to go ashore and later transferred to another ship to make the trip to Quebec. This leg of the trip took about a week.

Dietrich did not recall spending much time in Quebec. As a twelve-year-old, he did not know much of what was going on, but was mainly concerned with not losing sight of the family. In Quebec, they all boarded the Canadian Pacific Railroad and headed for Winnipeg. By this time, large sums of money were owed to the railroad by the travelers for their passage. After about twelve years, Dietrich was able to pay about twenty-five percent of the original charges. The C.P.R. had gradually reduced the price of the passage when it became obvious that, due to the depression, most former passengers would not be able to pay the full amount.

The local Mennonite churches were able to assist the new arrivals very little because most of the members were also recent emigrants from Russia. The Friesen family stayed in the nearby community of LaSalle, Manitoba, with church families for several months until they could get their own place. Dietrich's older brothers were able to obtain work harvesting grain on the farm. This was hard, cold work because an autumn flood had delayed the harvest and the grain was covered with ice and snow.

Dietrich entered school the day after they moved to LaSalle. He had ten cents to spend for supplies, and it was here he began his encounter with the English language. Though he was twelve years old, he started with grade one. In a few months, he moved to grade two. After that, he skipped to grade four and soon moved to grades seven and eight. At age sixteen he was ready to write the exams. High school was done in a more orderly fashion because the language was no longer a problem. He was not able to complete high school because he needed to help with the care of his mother, who was living with brother Abe in Winnipeg. Mother's health was failing at this time, and the boys gradually had to care for her physical needs as well as her financial ones.

Brother Abe worked as a shoemaker, but Dietrich was able to find work with a friend as a clerk in a grocery store. He made deliveries by bicycle, carrying loads on both the front and back of his two-wheeler. This was sometimes difficult through the snows of winter.

Dietrich became a Christian at the urging of his mother and was baptized at age 18 in a river south of Winnipeg. He became a member of the LaSalle Mennonite Brethren Church.

It was during this time that Dietrich and I became

acquainted, after meeting at the wedding of mutual friends. Dietrich's mother had already passed away by then. To Dietrich's family and friends there was nothing new and exciting about his new girlfriend, because her name was Annie—again—just like his brother Peter's wife and brother Jake's wife. Those boys believed that if one Annie is good, three should be better! So I was welcomed into the family in spite, or because, of my name.

Once, after I had returned to Margaret, Dietrich sent me a huge bouquet of gladioli—a big surprise to me and my family. On another occasion, he borrowed a friend's car and drove to Margaret to visit me and my family. Dietrich had already spoken of marriage, but was going to formally propose and talk with my parents. I had gotten one of the new Marcelle hairdos for the occasion. We went for a ride in the borrowed '32 Ford and ran into a rainstorm. The car got stuck in a ditch and we had to put all our finery aside and work to free the car. My hairdo was ruined, but wedding plans were still made.

NINE

Pre-Wedding Days

$\mathcal{J}$ came back to my parents' home in the early summer of 1936. I felt I need to earn the money for my wedding gown and accessories, so I found a job on the Patterson's farm, about thirty miles from home.

Mr. and Mrs. Patterson and their children were warm and pleasant. Their three-year-old daughter was severely asthmatic. The baby boy was nine months old and very heavy. I carried him around quite a bit and felt it.

In all my nineteen years, I had never worked as hard as I worked that summer. The day began at 5 AM. I stumbled and fumbled down the stairs every morning no more than half awake.

First I had to build a fire in the black cook stove. Crumpled up newspapers, dry kindling (brought in the previous evening), and several smallish pieces of wood was what it took. Then I would make the coffee in a percolator, put the water on for hot oatmeal, and fry slabs of thick bacon or ham. Lastly, I had to fry the eggs and make a mountain of toast.

After breakfast came the dish washing. Two large basins of water, one for washing and one for rinsing. We worked on the table, since they had no sink at that time.

Monday was wash day. They did have a motorized washing machine, so the wringer had to be turned by hand. By the time I got to the clothesline to hang the clothes to dry, I was exhausted. But then it was time to start cooking the main meal of the day.

This meal was usually boiled potatoes, some type of beef or chicken (the chicken had to be killed, dressed, and drawn by us), a salad of fresh garden greens, homemade bread, and, almost every day, a homemade pie for dessert.

My job was preparing the vegetables, cutting the bread, and setting the table, as well as helping with the children.

The evening meal was lighter than dinner. We called it *supper*. There were usually fried potatoes or noodles, and other leftovers, but always a dish of fruit and cake, which I would sometimes have to bake.

Doing the evening dishes, including the washing of the cream separator (the most distasteful job in the world, for at that time I still had my sense of smell) was a difficult chore for me. The milk strainer cloth and the milk pails were last. They had to be washed and rinsed and were usually hung upside-down on the fence posts near the kitchen door to dry. All day long they would gleam in the bright Manitoba sunshine, only to be filled again with the warm, frothy milk at the end of the day.

I also had to learn the intricacies of relieving the "Bossies" and "Rosies" of their generous supply of milk—not a coveted chore on hot summer evenings when the flies swarmed all over the cows and me. The only defense the cows had was switching their tails, and all too often it would strike my face and injury would be heaped on insult. I didn't want to be out there in the first place!

The churning of the sour cream was also a weekly chore. The churn in this case was a huge barrel in a metal framework, operated by a foot pedal which made the barrel swing back and forth. How longingly I listened for the swish and plop sound, which meant that the butter had formed.

The butter was then removed and immediately plunged into very cold water directly from the well. It was then handled with a wide, wooden paddle. The water had to be changed until all the milk was washed out of the butter. Finally it was pressed into a one-pound wooden mold, released from the mold onto wax paper, wrapped, and taken down to the cool cellar until it could be taken to the grocery store and exchanged for whatever goods needed to be bought. I believe it is partly due to the above processing of milk, cream, and butter that I cannot tolerate them to this day. Most of you know the only way I eat butter or margarine is when it's melted on toast, and then so sparsely that I can't identify it.

Ironing and bread baking usually fell on the same day, since the stove was fired up for the bread and the flat irons were hot. This also made the ironing very hot work.

I had learned to iron my father's dress shirts at age thirteen, so I enjoyed ironing day best of all. This was before ironing boards, which made it quite a challenge to iron skirts and dresses on the table.

By the end of each day, after all was said and done, I was so tired I could hardly make it up the stairs and to my bed, dreading the moment the alarm would shatter my sleep again at 5 AM.

I earned $8 a month that summer. Several factors throughout that long, hot summer helped me keep my sanity. They were that Dietrich was working on the farm adjacent to the Patterson's and we could see each other on Sundays, the excitement of our forthcoming marriage in October, and our upcoming move to make our home in Winnipeg—forever away from the farm!

HERE is the experience that Dietrich and I had the time we drove all night with horse and buggy to visit my parents:

We left our jobs on the farm after dark on Saturday night, driving through the back country along the river. It was more of a wagon trail than a road, with many sudden and unexpected turns, dips, and twists. Sometimes the trail led through thick bushes, up hill and down.

There is a certain hush during the hours between midnight and dawn. It is a feeling of security, for you cannot see anything beyond the immediate. It is as if you are enfolded within a safe, dark place that cannot allow anything to come near, and all you hear is the subdued voice of the night.

We were in a state of ethereal tenderness, far away from civilization, only the two of us in a one-horse buggy. What dangers may have been lurking in the deep woods? We sat very close, protecting each other, while the trusty horse clip-clopped along the unknown trail.

The hours leading to midnight were filled with sounds—birds busily and noisily finding resting places, owls hooting and, from far off, being answered. The feathered world was making love calls before it settled down for the night.

We were making plans for the future. Our hearts were filled to overflowing with young love. How promising everything looked to us. We felt so close in the impenetrable darkness, so sure all we hoped for would happen just as we planned and dreamed.

After midnight we could hear and sense the quiet all around us. We were kept awake as we bounced and were jostled about in the buggy. The horse seemed to follow the trail unerringly.

Just before the first glimmer of dawn, we began to hear

fluttering in the trees, then a chirp here and there. With the break of dawn, a cacophony of birdsong, almost too sweet to bear. It was like a symphony tuning up before a performance. We became involved in the beauty of it. The rosy morning, the cool invigorating air made us feel newborn.

Suddenly we saw before us a river—the trail ended on the river bank and started up again on the other side. The horse stopped and took a long drink of that clear, cold, sweet water. The riverbed was clearly visible and did not look very deep. With a little urging, the horse gingerly made her way into the water and we got across without mishap.

By six o'clock on Sunday morning, we drove into my parents' yard very quietly. The family was still asleep and we didn't quite know how to make our presence known to them. We unhitched old Nelly from the buggy and decided we would sing at my parents' window. Better than banging on the door, we thought.

My father's favorite song was "The Morning Light Is Breaking," which was appropriate for the dawn. So we tuned up our voices, even as the birds had taught us, and sang in German:

The morning light is breaking
The darkness disappears
The sons of Earth are waking
To penitential tears.

Each breeze that sweeps the ocean
Brings tidings from afar
Of nations in commotion
Prepared for Zion's war.
　　—George J. Webb, 1837

Our singing paid off, for soon my younger brothers and sisters were hurrying helter-skelter down the steep, dark stairway, each wanting to be the first to greet us.

Before long, Mother and Dad had the fire going in the kitchen range and, as always on Sunday mornings, Mother produced a big bowl full of delicious, golden *zwieback* and fragrant cups of coffee.

We all sat around the long oilcloth-covered table in our lean-to kitchen and enjoyed the fellowship with our loving family. Our hearts and minds were full of thoughts of our forthcoming marriage.

TEN

Our Wedding

And so the time arrived for our wedding, which took place on October 11, 1936, in the home of my parents.

In those days it was customary to have a shower (*polter abend*) for the young couple the evening prior to the wedding. And so it also happened for us. The shower included young and old, men and women, and always singing, playing guitar, and even some recitations. All of this was voluntary, and the guests came from far and near. After the gifts were opened and duly admired by all, it was time for good food and fellowship. I don't know how many *zwieback*, cookies, and cakes were served and eaten, but I know everything was enjoyed.

The gifts in those days were not anything like what we give and receive nowadays. No fine china, crystal, or sterling silver. I wish I could remember how many sets of cutesy salt and pepper shakers we received. They were the sole décor in our apartment for many years!

We also received sets of carnival glass dessert bowls, some of the pink glass and some of the green. You find them in antique shops and yard sales now, and my heart and mind always turn weak with nostalgia at the sight of them. A pair of home-sewn sheets made out of unbleached muslin was a prized gift. Towels were also wonderful and helpful. We felt like royalty with all the things we got, and I have always tried hard to make our home look pretty.

The joy and excitement I felt allowed me a deep sleep that Saturday night so long ago. At daybreak on Sunday, I stood shivering at the upstairs window in my parents' house in Margaret, Manitoba, expecting beautiful, golden sunshine. What I saw filled me with anguish. Heavy, leaden skies, not a chance of the sun coming through. The ground was frozen and it looked as if the clouds could bring snow.

Only yesterday it had been a warm, sunny day while we gathered green branches to decorate the wooden kitchen chairs we would sit on during our wedding ceremony. And today these ominous black clouds. And on our wedding day!

I was so young then, only nineteen, and had been so sheltered by living in rural areas, surrounded by doting parents and an array of both older and younger siblings. Now I was going to be married, leave my parental home, begin a new life, and make a home for my soon-to-be husband who was, in my heart and mind, the most admirable, handsome, and musically talented young man. We were so much in love.

Soon the hustle and bustle of the household and the many things that needed to be done took away the gloom of the dreary, cold day. My parents' home was already over-flowing with relatives and friends who had arrived from Winnipeg and other outlying areas. The house was deco-rated with greenery and blue and white paper flowers.

My family had prepared all the food for about 100 ex-pected guests. The custom at that time was that the bride's family mixed the dough for the *zwieback* and then took large batches of the dough to friends and neighbors who would bake the *zwieback* for the family. That was a great help for the hosts of the wedding.

The welcome aroma of freshly brewed coffee and Mother's delicious *zwieback* was everywhere. The bride-to-be, however, was in a state of euphoria all her own and could not be counted on for any culinary assistance!

THE midday meal on that Sunday was a wedding feast indeed! A young beef had been butchered for the event, and hours of preparation had gone into the huge kettle of delicious *borscht*, tender roasts, and, in true Menno-nite style, *katletin* (meat balls), which are so good served with homemade hot mustard and eaten along with the ever-delectable and traditional *zwieback*. And last but not least, the delicious *plumi mouss*, rich with dried prunes, apples, apricots, pears, and raisins, all simmered to plump perfection.

By two o'clock on that Sunday afternoon, I was dressed in a simple, long-sleeved, floor-length wedding gown of white crepe that had cost $8.98. The veil was borrowed from my sister Mary and had a circle of artificial orange blossoms and crepe myrtle. My white T-strap high heels had cost $2.98. My face was entirely void of makeup and I carried no bouquet. The flowers that adorned our black chairs I had made of blue crepe paper and they were entwined in the green foliage.

The excitement and joy I experienced on that day are indescribable. I could think only of walking down that short aisle arm-in-arm with my beloved to become his wife. When Dietrich arrived looking so handsome and majestic in his black pin-striped suit, white shirt, and traditional Mennonite-style white satin ribbon and crepe myrtle pinned to his lapel, my heart turned over with love and the thrill of this wonderful wedding day.

My hands were icy cold, my knees shook so I could hardly walk, and it seemed as if the familiar living room was as large as a cathedral. Chairs and benches everywhere all filled with smiling, happy friends. The wedding music was played by an elderly gentleman on the organ that I played daily and dearly loved. All through the long service, my shaking and trembling continued through several choir songs, three speakers (who all unknowingly used the same Bible verse ("Serve the Lord with gladness"), various recitations and good wishes from family and friends, until finally the knot was tied. Then I could relax and begin to see what was happening around me.

※

True Love

I found thee slumbering sweetly
Within the confines of my youthful heart,
There dids't thou dream and hope for one to come
That could awaken thee with his soft touch,
My dreams were close akin to thine, dear heart.

I'd yearned for one to come and part
The curtain that was veiling him from me,
And then he came, the one I'd waited for so long.
To waken thee from sweetest dreams
His touch was that of shimmering moonlit beams.
My heart and soul rejoiced in ecstasy
That my fond dream is now reality.

※

DIETRICH was always supportive and always expressed his pride in me. He knew how to make me feel good about myself. Even though we were poor as church mice, I don't think we ever felt it.

We spent the first night after our wedding in my parents' home, for on Monday morning, as was the Mennonite custom, many of our neighbors and friends came over for breakfast and expected the newlyweds to be there. So one more time it was a party where every last *zwieback*, sausage, ham, and cookie were consumed.

After the last guest disappeared, we packed up our newly acquired wealth and piled it carefully into an old 1929 Star, a car converted into a pickup without a top. Our parents wrapped us in warm, homemade patchwork quilts and tearfully sent us off on the 150 mile journey to Winnipeg to make our own way in life, a life that they knew would have its difficulties. But we were young and romantic and totally happy. It was a very cold ride!

The second night we spent at the home of Dietrich's brother Peter and his wife Annie in Oak Bluff, and we also went to his oldest brother John and Helen's house in La-Salle. I remember they gave us a small saucepan in which we cooked our daily portion of breakfast oatmeal for years.

The last leg of our journey was the most exciting, for we knew we had a place to live. Dietrich had arranged for this before he came for the wedding.

ELEVEN

North Kildonan

*O*ur rooms were upstairs in the Peter Fotes' house on Henderson Highway in North Kildonan, a suburb of Winnipeg. The Fotes' oldest daughter, Kay Isaak, and her husband John, who now live in British Columbia, are still our faithful, loyal, and devoted friends.

There was one room that served as living and bedroom. And another room, the tiniest room you can imagine in your mind, was originally built to be a bathroom without plumbing. There was room in there for the smallest wood burning stove you have ever seen (also the cutest) and two orange crates standing on end. One held the pail of drinking and cooking water that we had to carry from the pump in the neighbor's yard. The other crate held the wash basin. I was very proud when we had a few pennies so I could buy some inexpensive material to make little curtains to hang in front of those crates and also a little ruffle for the edge of the open shelf that held our four plates, cups, and saucers, and the fruit dishes and salt shakers. I had so much fun playing at housekeeping.

At this time, Dietrich worked for our close friend who owned a little corner grocery store just a few steps from where we lived. Victor and Anne Wilms had been married one year earlier. We spent a lot of time with them, and they were a big help to us. Dietrich, with his musical talent and abilities, was an inspiration to Victor and Anne. We have kept our friendship with them in spite of the years and distance that have separated us. When we get together, it is as if we have never been apart. They are true friends. I treasure friends among my most precious possessions.

Dietrich also started private studies in vocal music and theory with Ben Horch who, at that time, was minister of music in the North End Mennonite Brethren Church. In 1941 Dietrich himself became the director of that choir and the first one to be remunerated. He received $4 a month.

We lived in this upstairs room from October 1936 to May 1937. When we discovered that we were going to have a baby, we looked for another place to live. We found a sweet, little house, again in North Kildonan, that we rented for $6 a month. We had a living room, kitchen, bedroom, and pantry. The rooms were tiny, but they would be just right for three of us. How happy and excited we were anticipating becoming parents.

There was no plumbing. We carried water from a

community pump. We had electric light with the cord hanging from the ceiling. The proverbial "white house" was in among the trees behind the house.

Our little wood burning cook stove had a very small firebox, so it could not retain heat for long. During the winter nights, the house got so cold that the water in the pail or basin was frozen by morning.

It may interest you to know what we paid for things at that time: hamburger, 3 cents a pound; bread, 10 cents for 3 loaves; street car fare (round trip), 15 cents; Chinese food in a restaurant, 15 cents; cup of coffee, 5 cents; ice cream cone, 5 cents. Fabric for a maternity dress, which I sewed by hand, was 12 cents per yard.

Shortly before our first baby was born, Dietrich and I went to see the movie *Maytime*, even though the church frowned on its members attending movies. We were tempted beyond our strength and enjoyed the beautiful music and singing of Jeanette MacDonald and Nelson Eddie. They sang their way right into our hearts. What a musical treat that was for us!

It was during this time in my life that I learned to appreciate the cultural side of Winnipeg. The music of the opera *Carmen*, the ballet *Swan Lake*, the oratorio *Elijah*, conducted by the famous Arturo Toscanini, to name a few, were revelations and inspired my music-starved soul. We never missed the choral festivals held every spring, and I was privileged to sing in one of those choirs.

Katherine Rosamund

Katherine Rosamund, our sweet, beautiful and healthy baby girl was born in the Concordia Hospital in Winnipeg, Manitoba, on July 9, 1937. She was chubby, blue-eyed, dark-haired, and weighed a little over eight pounds. We were the happiest parents and enjoyed caring for our pretty little girl.

Since our house was so small, I washed the square flannel diapers outside under the beautiful shade trees. The round galvanized tub and washboard held no dread for me. How joyfully I scrubbed, rinsed, and hung the white diapers on the clothesline for the sun to bleach and the summer breeze to blow and dry!

The furnishings in our house were few at this time. Our kitchen table, which was given to us, was old and had a somewhat warped top. We bought four basic wooden chairs. Our sofa was actually a trundle bed with half of the springs pulled out that could sleep two. That was our bed and sofa while we lived upstairs at the Fotes'. But now we had a double bed in the bedroom. We had one feather comforter, a leftover from Dietrich's mother who brought it from Russia. I made a blue and white gingham cover for it. That served us for many years. I do not recall a dresser at this time, but I was quite good at turning cartons and crates upside-down and making my own dressers—with a pretty scarf on top. I was very, very happy!

I have always loved doing embroidery or any handiwork.

Sister Helen gave me an unbleached linen bedspread with a beautiful floral design stamped on it. I enjoyed embroidering it and used it on our bed for years.

Dietrich was always involved in church music, and by now he was taking voice lessons. For one special musical event, I got a new navy blue dress—short puff sleeves, a white collar, and a long wrap-around taffeta sash. It came with a navy blue taffeta slip. I wore a large-brimmed, white hat with this and felt as beautiful as the Queen of England. (Kathy has a black-and-white photo of me in this dress.) Kathy was about one year old at the time.

My sister Helen was working in Winnipeg then. She was quite fond of Kathy and spent a lot of time with us. Helen bought an elegant, burgundy-colored baby carriage for little Rosamund, as we all called Kathy then. It was an English perambulator, well-constructed with a metal body, leather upholstery, and a top you could put down.

In this comfortable, shiny, new carriage, Rosamund and I strolled on the streets of North Kildonan. Many an afternoon walk took us to visit the Victor Wilms, John De-Fehrs, John Koslowskys, and many other friends.

During the first winter, I wrapped Rosamund extra warmly, put her in the carriage, and let her take her afternoon nap outdoors in the lovely carriage. That was customary in those days.

Changing the diapers on winter nights was a challenge; it was a matter of speed! The steam from the wet diaper would rise up in a cloud while the big, blue eyes looked up at me. The baby shivered and shook, but never gave a cry. Then I wrapped her up snugly and tight and nursed her under our feather comforter where it was warm and soft.

At the time of this writing, Kathy and her husband Ed Robinson live in Fresno, California. Ed is retired from a management position with the J.C. Penney Co., and Kathy retired from her position as Executive Secretary to the President of Fresno Pacific College.

※

Mother's Day

The morning breaks at last, my senses reel.
The most exquisite gift lies in my arms,
A wondrous thing, such joy I feel
This tiny budding life—endearing charms.

This miracle of flesh and blood
So velvet soft and warm,
Prepares me now for motherhood.
God spare this child from harm.

With all my heart I dedicate my time
To nurture and to teach and love
This one who's brought me joy sublime,
And I implore the help of God above.

The years pass quickly—all too soon
They grow apart—and I?
The lullabies I used to croon
Change to a tear and sigh.

One by one, they've flown the nest.
I sit and rock and wait.
They tell me, "You deserve the rest,"
As they unlock the gate.

The flowers, the cards and gifts they bring
Make me feel loved and understood.
Above all else and everything,
Thank God for motherhood.

＊

IN early 1939 we left our dear little house and moved into a duplex on Kingsford Avenue. This was owned by Mr. and Mrs. DeFehr, Sr., parents to John DeFehr and his wife Helen, who, incidentally, were married just one week after our wedding.

This was a rather unique setting. The Sr. DeFehrs lived right in front of our door—Agatha and Emanuel Horch in the other duplex—with just a thin wall between us. John and Lydia Koslowsky were in the house next to the duplex, and John and Helen DeFehr in the house next to the Koslowskys. We had our own little social club. The

Koslowskys and Horches were married a year or so before us, so we were all pretty young.

While we lived here, we bought our first piano. How wonderfully exciting that was! Dietrich began taking piano lessons. He knew how much he would need that for his music career. At this time, he began to be the soloist for almost every wedding in the community. He also organized a male chorus, which served the church and various outlying areas for years. Often, when they were singing a special concert, he would ask me to sing the soprano obligato, which was an honor for me.

During the time we lived in this one-bedroom duplex (again without indoor plumbing), Sis, as we called my sister Helen, came over often, and it was Sis who first introduced us to chocolate chip cookies. At that time, the chocolate was in bar form and had to be broken into chunks. Our trusty little wood burning stove baked the first cookies for us, and how delicious they were!

It was also in this place that we invited friends other than immediate neighbors over for an evening's visit. Imagine my embarrassment when it came time to serve coffee and I had more guests than I had cups! I had to reach for some that were cracked, but it didn't keep me from entertaining. I found then that I loved to have people over, and outside of the three years during Dietrich's illness and death, I have entertained to my hearts' delight.

Coffee Break

The table is set, it looks so nice
The kitchen smells fragrant of sugar and spice,
Of chocolate and raisins and coconut, too.
All is awaiting the coming of you!

The tea cups are ready, the coffee is brewed,
The cookies still warm, I hope they'll be good.
I treasure your friendship, so please come along.
My heart is so happy, I'm singing a song!

It's been ever so long since last you were here.
A week or a month? It seems like a year!
We always store up the good things to say
And recall the tales of yesterday.

We'll chatter and laugh as our coffee we drink,
Of family, friends, and loved ones we'll think.
Some favorite recipes we'll happily share,
And life's experiences we'll compare.

The time passes quickly—we'll hug and embrace,
Remind each other of God's marvelous grace.
These intimate moments are precious and rare,
Our hearts overflowing—we'll whisper a prayer.

We had an intense social life in our own circle. Evenings, all the couples got together in one of our homes to play table games. Monopoly came in full force at that time, and we would sometimes play into the wee hours. The Wilms were always included, even though they lived several streets from our little village setting. Of course the hostess would always serve refreshments—homemade and delicious.

In the summer time, I would get up at five o'clock in the morning. On Tuesdays, ironing day, I would fire up the little stove and get a head start on my ironing. In the afternoon, we young mothers often had afternoon teas. We and the children would dress in our best and get together for a lovely time of fellowship and refreshments. Sometimes after eating all those goodies, we would hardly feel like going home to cook dinner for our hungry husbands, but we tried to plan ahead. In those days, though, not many of us had refrigerators, so it was always a challenge—what can we fix that will keep well?

During this time, I became pregnant again and experienced a near tragedy. I climbed up a ladder leading to the outdoor attic at the duplex. Suddenly the ladder slipped and I fell onto a pile of rocks below. My neighbor ran over to help me up, but I was fine. No harm at all.

Walter Herbert

Wally was born on October 2, 1939. Dietrich was auditioning to sing for C.B.C., so it was a busy and exciting night for us. Wally was the only child in our family to have the privilege of having his Grandma Warkentin help take care of him the first ten days of his life. That was a treat for me, too! I remember how much I enjoyed my nine days in St. Boniface Hospital, being waited on and having friends and my husband visiting. It was the *borscht* that Mother was cooking when we arrived home that made me realize that I had lost my sense of smell. She was dismayed that I could not enjoy the wonderful aroma of the fresh seasonings in the soup. I never have regained my sense of smell to this day.

Wally was a healthy, chubby, blond baby. He weighed almost ten pounds at birth. Such a nice armful of boy, and what a joy and delight to us. Again, Sis was quite taken with him, and when he was nine months old, she took him to see my parents in Margaret, Manitoba, a 150 mile train ride. I'm sure she had fun showing him off. She never had children of her own, so she could enjoy ours.

We lived in the tiny three-room house on Kingsford Avenue in North Kildonan that belonged to the DeFehrs. The other half of the house was the home of Agatha and Emmanuel Horch at that time.

We celebrated wonderful, wonderful Christmas Eves in North Kildonan. I still get thrilled at the remembrance of them. I sewed and knitted new clothes for the children, bought new shoes, and dressed them in warm snowsuits, scarves, and mittens. Then I tucked them into a hand-pulled sleigh and walked down the snow-covered streets. Usually there was soft, new snow falling on everything so that the fence posts looked like ice cream cones. The lights twinkled brightly and everyone was happy and joyful. Dietrich pulled the sleigh with my arm tucked warmly in his free arm. What a happy family we were.

The children's program in church—was there ever such angelic singing? With dear Tanta Anna in her glory and Wally trying his very best to outshine the other children. And, of course, in my eyes and heart, he surpassed them all.

I remember the first day of school for Wally. He was dressed in brown knickerbockers with leather patches on the knees. And I had knitted brown knee socks with a border of yellow horses. After all our farewells were said, Wally walked down McKay Avenue with Hänschen Spenst. After the final waves, and when I knew that he wouldn't turn to look again, I wept. I don't know how long I stood on the street and wept for the baby that seemed to be going out of one part of my life, the part where I could hold and hug and keep him to myself. That was a real severing of our hearts. But Wally came home so happy and excited, and I knew he was still mine.

At the time of this writing, Walt and his wife Dolly live in Lodi, California. Wally retired from the California Youth Authority and is presently developing a Victim-Offender Reconciliation Program in San Joaquin Valley. He also does volunteer counseling for the Salvation Army.

Dolly works part-time in the clerical department for the CYA Stockton Parole Office.

AROUND this time, Dietrich got a job working in the Klassen brothers' machine shop. These three Klassens were brothers to Anne Wilms. Dietrich's job was to run a press that punched washers out of tin. It was a noisy place and dirty work, but we were on cloud nine. His wages were $9 a week, so we could pay the doctor and hospital. Everybody always told me that Dietrich out sang the noise! He was known for singing in every situation. Indeed, he often would sing the things he was telling me.

The duplex soon became too small for the four of us. The Koslowskys decided to move into the city, so we moved into the bigger house. It had several bedrooms upstairs and another downstairs. The Sr. DeFehrs owned this house as well. So we moved into the big house and it was there that Wally fell against the hot end of the kitchen stove and burned his arm badly. How we all agonized over that burn. For a long time, he had a big blister, and then eventually a scab. Wally was also fascinated by the electrical outlets in that house and got shocked when he put his warm, wet fingers in them. We thought maybe he would be an electrical engineer some day!

Here we lived with our growing family. Mrs. DeFehr always had beautiful flowers and took great pride in them. John and Helen had a son, Leonard. He and Wally were the same age and often plundered Mrs. DeFehr's tiger lilies, because the buds looked like carrots to them. Mrs. DeFehr insisted that we tie the boys to a tree so they couldn't reach her flowers. She was so upset. We tried tying the boys up, but that was much too risky. So we just had to watch them more closely.

Wally and Leonard were two of a kind. There was the time the three-year-old lads decided to make their "Great Escape" and almost frightened two mothers to death! Especially when they were found on Henderson Highway on the other side of the subway. We were so relieved and happy to have them back safe and sound. Now they are still friends and, of all things, in the same type of work.

While we lived in the larger house, Dietrich's older brother Abe returned to Winnipeg from Ontario where he had worked for some time. It was soon decided that he would come and live with use, since he was still single at that time.

Abe was not settled in a profession as yet, but he was a shoe maker. This was the time he opened up a shoe shop, mainly fixing shoes, I believe, although in Russia he had also made shoes.

Abe loved our children, and at mealtime he usually had either Wally or Kathy tucked under his left arm and fed them while at the same time eating his own meal. He was very appreciative of my cooking. When I made a special dish for him on one occasion, called "Sweet Milk Mouss," he was so thrilled that he reached in his pocket and gave me a dollar. In the late 30s, that was special! So Uncle Abe endeared himself to all of us. Every one of our children is very fond of him.

In fact, it was during the time Abe stayed with us that he very excitedly asked us whether he could tell us a big secret. He had found a lady love. He brought Katie Martens over to our place so we could meet her. Since we approved of his choice, they became engaged. We were all quite fond of Katie.

Dietrich and I decided we wanted to have the engagement dinner for them. The extended Friesen family was invited, and I, to the best of my ability, cooked a meal for that occasion. Believe me, it wasn't gourmet. I recall having salmon loaf. I don't know what else was on the menu, but the dinner seemed to be a success. This was the fist time we had all the Friesen brothers and their spouses in our home. Really quite scary for me.

On September 26, 1941, Dietrich, myself, Kathy, and Wally were with my brothers, Frank and Allan, my sister Elsie, and my parents for the auction sale at their farm in Margaret, Manitoba, in preparation for their move to Clearbrook, British Columbia. They received $1,003 for their possessions and departed for Clearbrook on October 1.

In the fall of 1941, Dietrich was asked to take over the leadership of the North End Mennonite Brethren Church choir. This was very exciting and a challenging opportunity for him, and he accepted the position. The North End Church was in the city and, heretofore, had excellent music leadership in the person of Mr. Ben Horch, who was, at the time, considered to be the "father of all Mennonite choir directors." Dietrich and I had studied voice with him before we were married. The notable Mr. Franz Thiesen had also held the position of director of this choir.

Thus began our involvement with the people of the North End Church. The choir sang at both morning and evening services, and all services were in the German language. We immediately fell in love with all the choir members. We thoroughly enjoyed the music and gained many friends—friendships that have lasted up to this day. They all enthusiastically sang the way their new director led them. Dietrich had a wonderful sense of interpretation, much patience, and a gentle manner.

Since we did not own a car, we traveled by streetcar. This meant that we had at least a fifteen minute walk to the car stop, which, incidentally, was the end of the line. The streetcar came every fifteen minutes. Very often (mostly), we had to run half of that distance so we wouldn't miss it, but we were young then! Dietrich would take my hand and I would huff and puff to the best of my ability. I was wearing high-heeled shoes. I won no medal for speed but often think I deserved a Nobel Prize for courage! At Selkirk and Main Streets, we had to transfer. There was no shelter at that place. Whether it was sunny, raining, or furiously snowing and blowing, we huddled there until the right car came along. Oh, how cold we often got at that corner. This was our pattern, morning and evening on Sundays and Friday evenings for choir rehearsals. We did this for ten years with great joy and dedication.

However, that our dear children could not be with us was a painful realization. They were at home with a young girl taking care of them. When they got old enough to go to church, she would take them. The church in North Kildonan was in easy walking distance. How often I felt I should have been with them. It was not easy for me to leave the children so much, and I deeply regret not being there for them.

Victor Emmanuel

On December 18, 1941 our son Victor Emmanuel was born. So we had a Christmas baby! Another beautiful, healthy boy who got a lot of attention from his older siblings and a lot of special presents for Christmas. Three days later, Abe and Katie were married, on December 21, so I was unable to attend. Dietrich sang at the ceremony.

Vicky and I spent eight days at St. Boniface Hospital, bonding together and living in the luxury of being waited on, visited, and gifted—after all, it was Christmas! The hour when the nurse brought the baby to me was the most wonderful and satisfying time. I remember two gifts from friends that were given me. One was a flannel sheet with blue stripes at each end, and the other was a bag of the most delicious ripe pears I have ever eaten.

Our faithful babysitter, Agnes Fote, helped to take care of Kathy and Wally during my hospital stay. She decorated the Christmas tree for us. Agnes was a very efficient girl. Nothing seemed too much for her. She always had everything spic and span in the house. She helped us for years.

Vic was a strong, wiry boy. He was the only one of our six children who walked at nine months. I took him out of the crib one day, set him on the floor, and the next thing I knew he was following me around the room!

We had a near tragedy while we lived there. Vic, who was one-and-a-half years old, was in the backyard. I had to go down into the cellar for something, and when I came back up, Kathy was in tears trying to tell me that "Vicky drank something!" I could see him come staggering across the lawn, and by the time I reached him, he had collapsed. I took him in the house, and immediately our good and dear friend Mrs. Suderman came running over saying, "He drank kerosene. I can smell it!" (Remember that I had lost my sense of smell.) She heated some milk with butter in it and we tried in vain to make him drink this, but he was unconscious and didn't respond to our coaxing.

We decided we had to get him to a hospital. So, while Mrs. Suderman stayed with him, I ran down the street to the nearest neighbors who had a telephone and called Dietrich at the Klassen brother's machine shop. I told him, hysterically, of the situation. He came quickly, driving one of the big trucks the business used for hauling away tin.

We took the baby and literally bounced and jolted all the way to St. Boniface Hospital. Vic never opened his eyes on that long ride. Someone must have called the hospital, because when we arrived, the nurse was holding the door open for us. Everything was set up to pump Vic's stomach. Our doctor was there and went right to work getting that little stomach emptied. We were allowed to watch the whole procedure. The doctor and nurses all held their noses at the smell of kerosene.

We reluctantly left Vic at the hospital for an overnight stay so he could be watched for any complications. But he seemed as fine as could be the next day, and we thankfully and happily brought him home. We learned later that Vic had gone to the neighbor's garage, seen a small can of liquid and drank it. What a trauma that was for us.

Shortly hereafter, Vic began to have problems with sudden chills and would go into a high fever. I had often asked our doctor whether it would be advisable to take Vic's tonsils out, but he always said, "No, we don't like to do that before the child is at least three years old." But this time Vic was really very ill—his cheeks so red and his breathing rapid. We took him to the St. Boniface Hospital and discovered that he had kidney infection and pneumonia. The doctor beat his breast and said, "Why didn't I take out his tonsils sooner?" We had a very, very sick little boy. I wanted to stay with him, but the hospital wouldn't allow it. Later, we discovered that they hadn't expected Vic to live and didn't want a hysterical mother on their hands.

But live he did. Thank God for that. After we brought him home, we watched him very closely. The time I sat up with him all night, I went through the most dreadful agony. If Vic should die, I knew I would surely die of a broken heart. Suffering through this fear that time has given me a great compassion for parents who lose their children. Children are a part of us, and consequently we can't bear to know they are hurting in any way.

Shortly after Vic recovered from this illness, we had his tonsils removed. Our Dr. Klassen told me to be very careful about what Vic would eat. For a few days, he should eat only pudding or ice cream. But Vic defied that and begged for chicken noodle soup and dill pickles! We gave him exactly that, he thrived on it and was soon whole and hearty. What a blessing to have a healthy, robust boy again.

None of our other children had any major illness. We were so fortunate to have a healthy, well-adjusted family, and I can't thank the good Lord enough for such mercy.

At the time of this writing, Vic and his wife Darlene live in Fresno, California. Vic owns and operates a "Full o' Bull" submarine sandwich franchise in Madera, California, and Darlene is a divisional manager with Etna Insurance in Fresno.

WE built a new house on McKay Avenue in 1942. After we made the decision to move, we sold the house even though we had only enjoyed living in it for one year.

In 1943, Dietrich took over the Canadian Sunday School Mission Radio Choir, and for seven years held that position. There, too, I was in the soprano section. It had been forecast in a poem at our wedding that we would one day sing over radio. In a sense, this came true. Now we had three services every Sunday and an extra evening a week for rehearsal. Mode of transportation? Streetcar!

How exciting, when on the dot of 8:30 am every Sunday the little red light in the studio flashed on. Anne Penner played the arpeggio and we came on singing "Wonderful words, beautiful words, wonderful words of life."

Mr. Ken Robins was the radio speaker and Miss Anne Penner, the pianist. She also taught piano to Kathy and Wally, and became a very dear friend. There were usually around ten or twelve singers, and we sang wonderful gospel songs.

TWELVE

Clearbrook

It was during the war in the autumn of 1943, with many of the young men being conscripted into the military service, when we became concerned that Dietrich might be called to go. After much thought and prayer, we decided to move to British Columbia, where all my family lived by now, and where we could possibly work on the farm since farmers were exempt, even though farming was the last of the things either of us wanted to do. So it was that we sold our home on McKay and made preparations to move to British Columbia.

My younger sisters Susan and Elsie were planning to have a double wedding in Vancouver on October 9, and I wanted very much to be there. In order for that to happen, Kathy, who was six, Wally, four, Vic, two, and I would go in time for the wedding, and Dietrich would stay behind to wind up all our affairs. So began a very unforgettable train journey—a young mother, unaccustomed to traveling, much less with three small children.

We had a bag of provisions consisting of sandwiches, cookies, and fruit. No such luxury as going to the diner for us. I wonder how the food tasted after two days and nights on that Canadian Pacific Railroad train.

The children had the run of the train, and I mean run—up and down the narrow aisles! There were a lot of military men on board, and soon Vic was bringing me a soldier's cap, a box of cigarettes, candy bars, etc., which he picked up in passing. And it became my duty to take said articles back up the aisle and find their very amused owners—to my utter embarrassment and the children's delight!

The nights were a nightmare. We did have a sleeping berth, but the children were afraid of that small, dark space. So Mom spent most of those dark hours soothing one or the other of the children and wishing with all my heart for my husband's help.

For some reason that I don't recall, some of the passenger cars were left in Calgary, Alberta, just sitting on the tracks with nothing happening. I took advantage of this, and we all went out and scampered around in the fresh air.

By the time we arrived in Vancouver, I know I was a basket case. But I could also depend on my sisters and mother to relieve me once in a while and keep an eye on the children. My parents and my sister Helen had bought a very nice house with several bedrooms upstairs, so we all had adequate room there.

Susan and Elsie and their bridegrooms, both named John, were beautiful and handsome. Something usually has to go wrong at a wedding, and that evening it was the brides and bridegrooms who got lost on their way to the church and being half an hour late. The poor pianist who was playing the wedding music had to repeat her repertoire over and over, and the guests got quite restless. But finally they arrived and the ceremony could begin.

Although I thoroughly enjoyed visiting my family and many friends in British Columbia, I could not visualize us living or working on a farm. At that time, there was a lot of undeveloped land there, much of it with big, black burned out tree stumps that had to be removed by blasting. I was terrified at the thought of us starting on anything like that. Somehow, I conveyed this message to Dietrich who was still in Winnipeg. After much writing and telephoning, the decision was made that I would come back to Winnipeg and we would just make the best of whatever lay before us as far as the military draft was concerned.

Winnipeg Re-visited

I don't remember too much about our train trip back to Winnipeg, except that Wally got the chicken pox. But after a month of being alone with the children, I was eagerly looking forward to being at home with my husband. It was about the middle of November when we got back. How good it felt to all of us.

Dietrich had found a nice house for rent on Rose Street in North Kildonan. It had a living and dining room, kitchen, and two bedrooms. All but the kitchen had lovely hardwood floors. I spent a lot of time keeping those floors highly waxed and polished, but it never seemed like a chore to me.

That Christmas stands out clearly in my memory. When I awoke on Christmas morning, I felt something on my right arm. I reached over with my left hand, and I had a wristwatch on! Clearly Santa Claus had been busy that night. Dietrich had slipped it on my arm during my sleep and I never felt it. The sleep of the young! This was my first watch and I was thrilled.

Christmas has always been one of my favorite holidays, a special time of year. The hope of Christmas, the thrill of expectancy, the wonderful love that fills my being—it is in the air, all permeating, and delicious!

A Christmas in Canada brings to mind a fond memory. For weeks, I had written lists of the most desired, most glamorous, most unattainable gifts. Some that were unreasonable, some highly impractical—those would be the greatest fun. What woman wants to find an electric skillet or steam iron under a layer of soft tissue paper in a beautifully wrapped and ribboned box? Not me! I say, "Go for the romance, the most longed for!"

The day has come for us to do our Christmas shopping. The sparkle and glitter of the newly fallen snow adds to the excitement of our mood. The colorful lights reflecting in the whiteness of the snow seem to create illusionary fantasies.

We are headed for the city's most prestigious department store, The Hudson Bay. Every December it is resplendent in magnificent Christmas décor that brings a gleam and glow to even the darkest corner. Since we will do all of our shopping in this store, we decide to leave our coats, hats, and overshoes at the coat check counter so we will be more comfortable.

We spend most of the morning in the children's sports equipment. What exciting ways for children to play in the snow. We buy a sleigh, a pair of skates, a toboggan, and a pair of skis. How the children's eyes will sparkle and their feet fly when they take these out in the winter weather early on Christmas morning.

On this rare day, we indulge in a sit down lunch, relaxing and making plans for the rest of the day.

In those days, we could have all our purchases delivered to our home without cost, so we were not burdened down with carrying boxes and bundles while we continued our shopping.

After lunch, we parted company to explore further possibilities. The white, silk scarf and brown kid gloves I bought for my husband will enhance the look of his camel hair coat and make him even more handsome.

The gift I wish for myself the most is a muskrat fur muff. I am so overcome by curiosity and can't stop myself until I find them in various sizes and colors. Now I have high hopes my Santa will bring me one. To my great delight, this muff was secretly wrapped and tucked under the lowest branches of the Christmas tree.

It is twilight before we leave the wonderland of the store. Darkness comes suddenly. The railings and lamp posts are adorned with white filigree, and diamonds dance in the snow.

Bouncing and jostling in the ancient streetcar with shoppers crowding onto the plush green seats, we are homeward bound to our own hearth where we can dream our dreams and live in happy anticipation of our future years.

Summer Times

In the early forties, we had wonderful summer vacations. We did not own a car at that time, but the Victor Wilms did, so they were kind enough to include our family on their trips to Granite Lake, near Kenora, Ontario, just over the Manitoba border. Somehow we managed to pack ourselves all into one car: the Wilms kids, Ernest, Wanda and Viola, and our Kathy, Wally, and Vicky.

The log cabins were nestled in the mighty trees that surrounded the wide, deep lake. The setting was peaceful, serene, and majestic. Leaving the noisy, hot city of Winnipeg was a pleasure in itself. To enjoy the cool and clean atmosphere was blissful.

Don't think we had running water or indoor plumbing. Oh no! The proverbial one-seater in the back of the cabin was well hidden by the trees.

We brought everything from home—sheets, pillows, blankets, towels, soap, dishes, and food. And such delicious food—bread, *zwieback*, cookies, butter tarts, and *pereshki* to name a few.

The first day was taken up with settling in. We had a cabin for ourselves, so we made up beds and decided where everyone would sleep. The nights got cold and the days were sunny and hot enough to give us terrific sunburns. I suffered my first and only sunburn on that lake, and I hurt for a long time.

Our supper on the day of arrival was usually prepared at home. But breakfast the next day was cooked lake side on an open fire. Never has anything tasted better! Huge skillets of fried potatoes, ham or bacon, and perfectly fried eggs, always cooked by Anne Wilms. (As you know, to this day I shy away from frying eggs!) Coffee perked on the blazing fire—oh, the delight of it!

When the day got warmer, the children would be so anxious to go swimming. To see those little bodies in that huge lake was frightening to us mothers. Many a time one of the daddies had to jump into the water for a quick rescue. And you ask why mothers get gray!

The boating was also hazardous. All those children jumping up and down, and our husbands often rocked the boat just to tease and frighten us—all in fun, of course.

One day the men went to another lake to catch some fish. Victor had a motor on his boat. After they caught their quota, they lost the motor in the deepest part of the lake, much to their horror. They got help in trying to locate the motor, but it was never found.

But the fresh fish fry that evening was delectable. Golden brown, fried in butter, and eat as much as you can.

On weekends, John and Helen DeFehr and family would join us, along with Victor's sister Agnes and her husband John Neufeld.

After the children were tucked in for the night, we would sit around the outdoor fire and swap stories and generally be tormented by huge, hungry mosquitoes.

What I remember most about Granite Lake is the tranquility and sense of peace it afforded during the hot summer months. To the city dwellers, it was restful and serene. In its unruffled, placid surface, the reflection of the surrounding trees and foliage gave the appearance of a dark green border around its glassy depth. Just before dawn, the morning vapors and mists hung low over the lake's stillness, as if to hide the secrets buried in its bosom.

After the sun scaled above the trees, the lake shone and glistened like a mirror—clean, smooth, and undisturbed. It was when the campers rowed the boats away from the shore that the stillness was shattered. Men and boys, shouting and laughing, racing and rocking the boats. Motors and oars churning the water until it heaved and foamed. The older children ran and splashed each other, fell and jumped off the wooden pier, their screams and cries echoed across the lake.

The mothers anxiously watched the little girls in their ruffled tops and bloomer bottoms, while the little boys seemed bent on ducking, pushing, and drowning each other.

After nightfall, the lake was a mystery clothed in black velvet, supple and soft. We heard the silence, with only a whisper of shallow waves lapping on the now silent shore. With the rising of the full moon, the lake became a shimmering, gleaming jewel that brought peace to our hearts and wonderment to our souls. It is God alone who created such miraculous beauty for us to enjoy.

Toward the end of the war, in 1945, Dietrich began teaching music at the Winnipeg Bible Institute and at Winkler Bible Institute, about 70 miles south of Winnipeg. He made this trip once a week by train or bus, teaching private voice students on the evening of his arrival and choral classes the following day. He also took some further studies in music at the Mennonite Brethren Bible College in Winnipeg.

Allan Orlando

Allan Orlando was born on October 24, 1946. At that time, we lived on McKay Avenue in a rented house—two bedrooms upstairs where the children slept and one downstairs for us and the new baby. There was no indoor plumbing. All the water had to be carried from the pump across the street—a treacherous job in the cold of winter when ice would form all around the pump. There was a cellar under the kitchen that we could never use because it was always flooded due to having no cement on the floor or walls. When it rained, the water collected in the cellar. I had a terrible fear of that watery hole under the house.

I had prepared extra food and baked goods for the time I would be hospitalized with my baby. I remember baking a large batch of ammonia cookies. While I was in labor at the hospital, the doctor came by on his rounds, about 5 PM, and decided to give me a shot to speed up the delivery. I heard him tell the nurses that he was going to a concert and wouldn't want to be late. So, in short order, Allan was born, a beautiful, healthy boy with long dark hair and dark, rather thick eyebrows and lashes—taking after my Mother Wiebe's side of the family.

After I was in my room that evening, coming out of the ether or chloroform used as an anesthetic during childbirth, I began to have a severe headache and soon began to tremble. Finally my whole body shook uncontrollably. I began to scream for help. After what seemed an eternity to me, nurses came running and gave me something which finally stopped the convulsions. That was a frightening experience and troubled me for months after. I believe it was the result of bringing on the delivery too soon.

When Allan was about one year old, we bought a house at 208 Oakland Avenue that had a pump at the back door. This was indeed a luxury. We also had a cement basement that had a coal-burning furnace and a shelf-lined storage room to keep all our jars of canned fruits, dill pickles, and vegetables. There was also room to hang laundry to dry in the winter, which was truly a wonderful help.

It was due to gas escaping from the furnace that Allan and I almost died of asphyxiation one winter day. It was on a weekday when Kathy, Wally, and Vicky were at school, and Dietrich was at the college. I began to get sick with a headache so severe that I had to go to bed. Allan was taking his afternoon nap. We both slept until the children came home from school. They came to my bedroom and woke me, saying it smelled funny in the house. I realized then that it was gas from the furnace and sent the children to call our neighbor. She entered the house, yelling, "Oh my God, you're going to die!" She opened all the doors, grabbed Allan, wrapped him in a blanket and ran outside. As soon as the fresh air came into the house, I began to have the dry heaves until I thought my body would tear to pieces. When the doctor came, he said that a short time more and Allan and I would have died.

That was an unforgettable experience, but Allan and I seemed to be none the worse for it. Again, the Lord was watching over us.

At the time of this writing, Allan and his wife Christine live in North Highlands (Denver), Colorado. Allan is a consultative relationship manager for Imperial Wallcoverings. Christine works in the accounting department of the Highlands Ranch Community Association.

Dietrich's studies were completed in five years and included an Associate of Arts degree from Toronto Conservatory of Music. All this time, he was teaching music and directing choirs to support his family of four growing children.

In the spring of 1948, as a result of this intense schedule, Dietrich suffered a physical breakdown requiring bed rest for a couple of weeks. He was barely able to complete his classes, but did not lose any credit for his studies. This happened after Dietrich directed a mass choir at a song festival in Winnipeg.

The day Dietrich graduated from Winnipeg Bible College, June 30, 1950, was a momentous time for us. We had not anticipated any major changes in our lives as a result of this graduation, but when a faculty member inquired as to Dietrich's plans for the future, the answer was to basically continue his teaching in Winnipeg. This friend then encourage Dietrich to get a Bachelor of Arts degree, and suggested that Tabor College, the Mennonite Brethren college in Kansas, might be the place where he could get the most credit for the work already completed. This was indeed a brand new idea. But it did not take long for it to hit home and begin to grow.

By the time we were on our way home, Dietrich's mind was made up. Yes, this could be a possibility. Riding in the streetcar, he told me of this plan. I turned, looked into his face and said, "You are crazy!" He didn't even flinch. Plans were made to move to Hillsboro, Kansas.

We had bought a house, had four children, a wonderful church choir, many voice students, a host of close friends—and Dietrich only said, "Yes, I think it will work. We can be ready by September!"

Did we begin to scramble and prepare for this major move? No. Instead, Dietrich was scheduled to leave for the country where he was to being six weeks of choir clinics in churches of the outlying communities with a 150 mile radius of Winnipeg—Morden, Winkler, Steinbach, Boissevain, Elm Creek, and LaSalle.

We were sitting at the breakfast table the day after Dietrich completed this assignment when there was a knock on our door. A man we knew had heard that we might want to sell our house. He looked at it, said he would buy it, and did! Then we began to scramble! Selling things, giving things away, throwing away things, even lending things to friends until we would return to Winnipeg—

which we planned to do. But that was not what God had in mind for us.

So it was that in September 1950, the house in Winnipeg, as well as the furniture, was sold for a profit that helped to support our family while Dietrich was a student. Dietrich made a large wooden crate that contained our belongings, and it was sent by train to Tabor College in Hillsboro, Kansas.

THIRTEEN

America

Hillsboro, Kansas

In early September 1950, we arrived by train in Harrington, Kansas, with our crates, boxes, Magnavox (combination record player and radio), and, of course, our classical music records. Henry and Anne Baerg picked us up late in the evening and put us up for the night, making us feel welcomed and comfortable.

Coming from Winnipeg to Hillsboro was a delightful change. Suddenly we were immersed in a small, country town—no streetcars, no bus lines, and everybody knew everybody. We loved the warmth and informality of that environment. Oh, they teased us about our short, clipped Canadian accent, but we took that all in stride and soon adopted the Kansas drawl.

Those two years in Hillsboro were very informative as

to adapting to the United States lifestyle, which was more informal and relaxed than the life we had known in Winnipeg. We found the people friendly and warm, and we formed many lasting friendships, both in Hillsboro and Durham. Our children were readily accepted and loved by our friends, and many a swim party was enjoyed by all, along with picnic baskets bulging with food.

Upon our arrival at Hillsboro, we settled into an apartment at Tabor College, first in South Hall and eventually in North Hall. We became house parents in North Hall and thoroughly enjoyed supervising twenty young boys. They were lively and full of energy. When they heard the city fire alarm in the middle of the night, we soon heard twenty pairs of boots scrambling down the stairs in pursuit of the fire engine!

On Wednesday evenings, we had a devotional time with the boys and served homemade cinnamon rolls, cake or cookies, and coffee, which they enjoyed. Today, most of these men are pastors, teachers, businessmen, or musicians.

Our children grew in this environment for the two year it took Dietrich to complete the bachelor's degree study, which he did in 1952. During the summer months, Dietrich added to the family income by painting houses in the community.

Dietrich longed for a rest from directing a church choir, but our cousins Henry and Anne Baerg had other plans for us. Henry was the pastor of the Baptist church in nearby Durham, and the church needed a music director. So it happened that our family lovingly became involved in the activities of that small church. We experienced such a homey, loving reception there. Those dear people virtually carried us in their arms.

When we announced my pregnancy in the late summer of 1951, the baby and I became the center of attention. I was carrying a baby and they wanted to be part of the joy and excitement of it.

In January 1952, the ladies gave a marvelous baby shower for us with many lovely and useful gifts for the baby.

Eugene Mark

On Sunday, February 17, 1952, our fifth child was born in the Salem Hospital in Hillsboro, delivered by Dr. Janzen— Eugene Mark, the name by Dietrich and approved by me. Fair-haired and petite, he weighed in at 8 pounds and a few ounces. Eugene was a quiet, peaceful boy and was soon the little king in our family, loved by Kathy, Wally, Vicky and Allan, who were all helpful in caring for him. When he was six weeks old, we took him to church, and there, too, he got a lot of attention and love.

As of this writing, Eugene and his wife Wendy live in Townshend, Vermont. Eugene is a professional cellist, traveling worldwide with the Paul Winter Consort. Wendy is a full-time mother and also writes travel articles for various publications.

During our two years in Kansas, Dietrich also attended classes in Wichita, taking credit toward a Master's degree. Three days a week, in the mornings, he taught high school band in Durham, eleven miles north of Tabor. These were two wonderful years, and we made lifelong friends as I cared for Dietrich and the children and, at the same time, learned how to live and act like an American.

Fresno, California

Most of the requirements toward the M.A. in music from the University of Kansas in Wichita were completed when Dietrich was asked to teach music at the emerging Pacific Bible Institute and also be the minister of music at Bethany Mennonite Brethren Church in Fresno, California. We felt these were wide open doors, God's way of leading and directing our lives, and we decided to follow where He led us.

The family belongings were packed into a trailer. We did not move any furniture, except for a brand new RCA radio and phonograph, a large console model. We started our long journey to California in our 1948 Chrysler. The children were placed into the car, four in the backseat and six-month-old Eugene on my lap, plus baby paraphernalia and lunch fixings for the family in the front.

By the time we got as far as Kingman, Arizona, we were all pretty hot and exhausted. We stopped there for dinner and were on our way again by 6 PM, driving west with the sun blazing directly in our faces. It seemed none of us were happy, least of all the baby. He began to cry, and nothing I did could stop him. Believe me, I tried everything! By the time we got through the red rocks of Hoover Dam, we were all but blinded by the burning red sun in our eyes, almost desperate.

When we finally drove into Boulder City and saw green lawns and motels, we stopped at the first motel, scrambled out of the hot, crowded car and into the room. I fixed a cool bath for Eugene, put him on a cool, clean pillow, and he fell asleep, sleeping peacefully all night long. In the morning, we continued our trip and all was well again.

We arrived in Fresno on August 13, 1952, in 100 degree weather. We were warmly welcomed in every sense of the word. We spent the first three weeks in Pacific Bible Institute's married-student housing before we located and rented a house of our own on Grant Street.

The Bible Institute was small in the beginning, and almost every student was a part of the choir. Theory classes and smaller groups made up the rest of Dietrich's class load. We soon loved the faculty, staff, and students at the school and loved to have them come to our home for parties, recitals, and dinners. I felt it was a great blessing to share in these activities. The Lord blessed the ministry of music in the college for all the twenty-seven years we served.

DIETRICH still had some class work to complete at the University of Kansas, so in the summer of 1953 the family, with the exception of Kathy who was almost 16, headed back to

Kansas in the 1948 Chrysler. The Chrysler made it only to Dalhart, Texas, where the connecting rod malfunctioned. Dietrich traded it for another Chrysler that took us on to Kansas. In Kansas, he traded that car for a 1951 Desoto.

The courses for the Master's degree completed, we drove back to California, this time without any car trouble, and returned to the house on Adoline that the school owned.

In August of 1953, the day after we returned to Fresno from Hillsboro, Kansas, we left for Clearbrook, British Columbia. Dietrich's student visa and my visitor's visa were expired, and we needed to work on our immigration visas. Since almost my entire family, as well as Dietrich's brother and his wife, Abe and Katie, lived in Clearbrook, we were able to divide our family into their different homes. We then began countless trips to the Customs and Immigration office in Vancouver. We would get one requirement done and then find out that two more were needed. The affidavit of support arrived from Uncle Victor and Aunt Renetta Friesen in Hillsboro, but, alas, Allan's name was omitted. Another phone call and wait for the affidavit to be renewed. So much red tape and requirements, each one taking another trip to Vancouver.

Meanwhile, it was September and school was starting. We enrolled Kathy, Wally, and Vic in the school on Clearbrook Road and Old Yale Avenue. We were able to rent a two-bedroom cabin where we camped with our four children—living out of our suitcases of summer clothes while the season changed and rain poured day after day.

The cabin did boast a kitchen range but, to our chagrin, it was a sawdust burner. According to the dampness of the sawdust, the fire would or would not burn. You can imagine that with pouring rain every day, we had mostly "would not" days! This was a stressful time.

❁

Sawdust Burner

The little house was damp and cold,
But "there's a heater," we were told.
No wood in sight, no not a splinter
To modify this long, harsh winter.

How could we then heat up this place
So that its warmth would us embrace?
A scuttle full of sawdust on the side,
Its contents with disdain we eyed.

So find some paper, strike a match
And pour the sawdust down the hatch.
We watched and waited for some heat
But soon we made a fast retreat.

When smoke enveloped every turn
How sorely then our eyes did burn.
We fled that house—near death, and choked,
To central heat we're clearly yoked.

＊

THE next obstacle came in October. Wally had his twelfth birthday and now required a passport, which meant more urgent phone calls to Ottawa, Ontario, and another two-week wait for that document.

To the praise of our family and friends, I must say that they were wonderfully helpful and generous with us. Many a delicious chicken dinner, *borscht* or noodle soup, awaited us in their warm and dry homes. I will be forever grateful to all of you.

IT wasn't until the beginning of November when the im-migration office had every bit of information and history and we finally got permission to leave. We joyfully left for our home, our work, and school in Fresno where classes had already begun in September. We were royally wel-comed at Pacific Bible Institute, as well as Bethany Church where Dietrich was minister of music.

We settled into our house on Adoline Avenue and re-sumed our normal, happy life.

Work at Pacific Bible Institute continued to be Dietrich's main occupation, but church choirs filled many hours. Some of the other churches in which he conducted choirs include Reedley Mennonite Brethren, Armenian First Presbyterian, and Millbrook United Presbyterian.

Milton James

Our family also grew at this time with the arrival of our sixth child Milton, the only native Californian. On a lovely day in the spring of 1954, May 11, our fifth son, Milton James, was born at Fresno Community Hospital, weighing in at almost ten pounds—healthy, dark-haired, and good-natured! Compared to an average seven pound baby, Milton looked like a three-month-old—a cuddly armful.

Dietrich was on tour with the PBI choir in Oklahoma, Kansas, and Nebraska, precariously near to the baby's birth, so our precious friends Henry and Betty Friesen kept close watch over me until Dietrich's return.

We were on the way to Dr. James' office for an appointment when I began to have labor pains. Dietrich took me into the office but had to go back to the college to finish his teaching. I waited for awhile and the pains kept on. I then told the nurse, who whisked me into a room and called the doctor. He gave me one look and said, "Get her to the hospital, now!" Since Dietrich wasn't there, the nurse walked me across the street to the hospital and I was admitted, but not before we heard the screeching of brakes. It was Dietrich hurrying to be at my side. One hour later, we had our son in our arms. What a precious bundle!

The summer of 1955, when Milton was one year old, we went to Clearbrook to visit my parents. After two full days of driving, we arrive at Abe and Katie Friesen's shoe shop, put Milton on the floor where he forthwith, totally uncoached, took his first steps! How surprised we all were, and Uncle Abe immediately fitted him with a pair of white high-topped shoes.

※

Prayer for the Children

Take them in your arms today,
Hold them to Thy breast,
All their fears will melt away,
Their souls will be at rest.

Our finite hearts and helpless hands
Cannot reach out to meet their need,
But Thou who rules o'er all the lands
Will surely nurture, clothe and feed!

※

WHEN Milton was three years old, we lived on Norris Drive West in the Mayfair area. I was babysitting three-year-old Steve Neufeld at the time. The two boys got along well. One morning around nine o'clock, they were playing in the backyard with their stick horses.

Unfortunately the backyard was too constricted for

their travels, so they happily rode away and disappeared from my sight. I searched the neighborhood thoroughly but no one had heard or seen them. I then called Dietrich at PBI and he got some manpower together to go on a search. When the boys' stick horses were found close to the full-flowing canal near our home, our fears were multiplied.

A radio station was called and the disappearance of the two boys was soon announced. I was at home watching, praying, and waiting.

Finally at 1 PM, I got a call from Steve's father at his job. Steve was found outside of his home by the neighbors. Soon after I got a call from a city policeman who had found Milton walking on North Maroa Street. He was on his way home. Oh, what joyous relief!

When they arrived at home Milton was proudly standing on the front seat next to the policeman and pointing excitedly to the gun in the car.

The boys' version of the story goes something like this: They threw their stick horses into the water and then walked from Mayfair to Clinton Avenue, stopping to play in the goldfish pool at Veteran's Hospital. At some point, a lady in a blue dress put them on a bus, after which a policeman gave them a ride on a motorcycle. We will never know what really happened, and I hope that we will never experience such agony again.

All in all, the boys had strayed about five miles, but

they were both just fine and I continued to baby-sit Steve very, very watchfully!

At the time of this writing, Milton and his wife Bendta live in Fowler, California. Milton is the minister of music at the First United Methodist Church in Visalia, California. Bendta is a neighborhood resource center coordinator for the Fresno School District.

※

For the Love of My Children

How still it is when I'm alone,
Since all our children left our home.
The fridge is opened just by me
With no one here to share my tea
Or cookies, zwieback, jam or bread
Or maybe cinnamon rolls instead.

No jeans to patch or buttons to match,
My laundry now in two small loads.
Don't have to watch the pockets for toads
Or worms or nails or strings
Or all the favorite boyish things.
But oh how sweet to reminisce

'Bout all the childhood things I miss:
The sounds of "Happy Farmer" played
By hands that future skills displayed;

The trumpet notes resound anew
With blurps and bubbles, not a few.

The violin plus strings and bow,
Its whereabouts? I do not know.
The clarinet, a short term stay,
Has also gone its soundless way.

Then there's the cello, often towed
O'er land and sea or dusty road.
The voices singing, strong and sure,
Uplifting, joyous, and secure
Will keep on ringing loud and clear
To bless my heart from year to year.

⸙

Impatience

Play me a melody
Of memory—
Chubby grubby fingers
Awkwardly stretching,
Counting mechanically,
Sound of play,
Bouncing-dribbling,
Coming in through
The open door,

Eyes anxiously watching
The owlish clock,
Its hands crawling
Snail-like
Across the minutes,
Ball and cap,
Expectant,
Beside the chair.

＊

Pacific Bible Institute

At Pacific Bible Institute, Dietrich carried the main responsibility for the music program, assisted by part-time organ and piano instructors.

In the early 1960s, PBI moved from the old buildings downtown to a new campus in southeast Fresno and became Pacific College. With this move came full—time additions to the music department in order to expand the instrumental music program.

During his tenure at Pacific College, Dietrich enjoyed a semester sabbatical auditing music at the Vienna Academy of Music and Arts. He enjoyed participating in the performance of Haydn's *Creation* under the direction of the famous German conductor Hans Swarovsky. Dietrich enjoyed living in Vienna because of its historical significance to music. Many composers had their roots in Vienna, which served as a source of great music for centuries.

Accompanying us on this European trip were our two youngest sons, Eugene and Milton. We were able to visit other smaller European cities before returning home for the Christmas holidays, where he resumed duties as head of the music department at Pacific College

DIETRICH's life was dedicated to church music, and his main purpose was to witness and encourage its growth. Occasionally, the Bible Institute and various church choirs combined to perform larger works. One such event was the performance of *The Holy City*, by A.R. Gaul, accompanied by an orchestra. I was privileged and honored to be a soloist in this work. Handel's *Messiah*, Bach's *Christmas Oratorio,* and others followed.

This led to the formation of the Oratorio Society in the mid-1960s under Dietrich's leadership. The Society drew participants from the larger Fresno community and sometimes involved over 100 persons. The Society generally performed two concerts a year and met on Tuesday evenings for rehearsals. In the latter years, an orchestra of about 35 instrumentalists was included. The culmination of the Oratorio Society coincided with Dietrich's retirement from Fresno Pacific College in 1978. The final work was Faure's *Requiem*, presented at the First Congregational Church of Fresno.

With retirement also came a lessening of responsibilities in church music programs. One of his last services for the larger Mennonite constituency was conducting the

500-voice West Coast Mennonite Men's Chorus. This concert was presented in conjunction with the West Coast Mennonite Central Committee Relief Sale.

Dietrich began his music career in Canada in 1939 by directing a small male chorus and ended his career in California in 1979 by directing much larger groups. His career spanned forty years of service, primarily to the churches of the Mennonite Brethren Conference.

The freedom to travel was one of the benefits of retirement, and we were able to travel to New York and other major cities to follow the music careers of our younger sons. We witnessed a number of premier performances of the Paul Winter Consort, of which Eugene has been a part for many years. Most of those performances were in the St. John the Divine cathedral in New York City.

We have taken many trips to New York City. In the early 1960s, we were there for a week when Dietrich was taking a music course taught by Peter Willhowsky. We visited the United Nations, took a boat trip to the Statue of Liberty, saw musicals, and went to Rhode Island to hear the Metropolitan Opera perform *La Traviata* and *La Boheme*. We took a tour of the Bowery, saw the Broadway show *Annie*, and the Christmas Spectacular. We also watched the lighting of the Christmas tree in Rockefeller Center, saw the garment district, and drove through Harlem. New York is truly an awesome city, both terrible and wonderful.

❖

New York in December

New York, New York, with your Christmas décor,
You are more brilliant than ever before.
The wind blows cold on Rockefeller Square,
I shiver in ecstasy with snow in my hair.

The church of St. Patrick and St. John the Divine,
Stalwart and ancient in years of time.
Joys and sorrows within these walls
And many fervent and tearful calls
To heal the sick and bind their wounds,
Each spire and steeple with prayer resounds.

New York, New York, how majestic you seem,
Your magnificent structures like crystal they gleam,
Your towers and bridges built of steel
With acres of concrete and miles of wire
Reaching onward and upward to tallest spire.

New York, New York, the most awe-filled place,
Teeming with people of every race
Of creed and color, shape and size,
But all beloved in our Maker's eyes.

❖

Photos

Anne's father
Cornelius Peter Warkentin
British Columbia, circa 1950

Anne's mother
Katharina (Wiebe) Warkentin
Clearbrook, B.C., circa 1960

Anne and her siblings,
Zeneta, Saskatchewan, 1929.
L to R: Allan, Elsie, Susan,
Frank, Anne, Neal, Helen,
Mary.

Anne with her mother in
front of the same home in
Zeneta, a few years later.

*Anne and Dietrich
near the day of
their wedding,
Margaret, Manitoba.
1936.*

*Anne and Dietrich
circa 1945*

*Anne's family,
Fresno, California,
1962.
L to R: Diana, Vic,
Kathy, Allan, Dolly,
Wally, Anne, and
Dietrich. Seated:
Eugene, Milton.*

*Anne and Dietrich
at their 40th wedding
anniversary party in
Fresno, California, 1976.*

*Anne and her siblings
in Clearbrook, British
Columbia, 1988.
L to R: Mary, Tena,
Helen, Anne, Susan,
Elsie, and Allan.*

Anne and her children.
L to R: Walter, Anne, Kathy, Victor, Milton.
Seated: Eugene, Allan.

Anne Friesen
signing copies of her memoir, "With Love, Anne"
at her 80th birthday celebration,
March 1997, Fresno, California.

FOURTEEN

Siblings

No other sisters could have had more fun than we did. The tears and laughter mingled is what life is all about. I shall always remember those special times.

⚜

Sisters Reunion (1984)

Six sisters as different as east is from west,
Six sisters each in her own way the best,
Six sisters together the first time in years
With a great deal of laughter, a good many tears.

There's Mary the cook, the "doer and maker"
Of pereshki, pfeffernuts, and platz, the baker.
Her house is immaculate, we all know that,
And she's ready to feed us at the drop of a hat.

Tena is quiet in her own dear way.
She watches us carefully with little to say.
Her brain power is ticking, she uses tact,
Just ask her and she will supply the fact.

Helen has knowledge stored up in her brain,
For years I have tried that, but all in vain.
She remembers dates and times and things
That would fill a castle built for kings.

Susan now virtually our Miss Cheerful,
Listen to this and you'll get an earful.
Her talents are many and varied, you'll see,
A "pinpoint" on a picture she doesn't want to be.

Elsie the youngest surprised us all
By working in raspberries from spring to fall.
She treats everyone with loving care,
There's never a burden too heavy to bear.

And Anne—the one who can't type or sew,
All of her faults you already know.
But the one thing I'd like to tell you here
To me, you are all most precious and dear.

＊

Tale of Two Sisters *(1985)*

If I had a sister that lived down my street,
I'd put on the coffee and turn up the heat,
Press my nose against the window glass
And watch and wait until time could pass.

I'd scurry around and make everything neat,
Get so excited I'd fall over my feet.
If I had a sister for Christmas to come,
I would polish and shine up my entire home.

My china cups and a pitcher of cream,
If I had a sister come—that's my dream.
Cookies and candy, zwieback and jam,
That's the kind of a girl I am.

I'd think of the most wonderful things we could say.
We would laugh and talk, knit and crochet.
If one of my sisters would visit me,
The happiest woman I'd surely be.

I'd don my white apron and put on my smile
And rush to the window to wait there awhile.
If I had a sister that lived down my street,
I'd put on the coffee and turn up the heat.

Tena has Mary, and Mary has Tena,
That leaves three, Sue, Elsie, and Lena,
While Annie is waiting to turn up the heat,
Will one of my sisters come to live on my street?

A Tribute to Mary Durksen

My sister who died of cancer on October 4, 1992

Mary's home was impeccably clean; she was always on the warpath with dirt. Her laundry and linens were the whitest and brightest, and her shelves and dresser drawers were organized and neat. She worked hard in whatever she did. Usually she was a step ahead of everybody else, a leader and "can do" person.

Mary was an excellent cook, majoring in old-fashioned foods. Her baked hams and chicken wings were succulently delicious. Her *plumi mouss*, thick with dried fruits of many kinds, was rich and delectable. Her *zwieback* and ammonia peppermint cookies were ever present, light and fluffy and oh so good. Her homemade chicken noodle soup, *verenika,* and gravy were unsurpassed.

Hospitality was her forte—no matter when we arrived at her home, ever ready was a cup of coffee and luscious pastries. Although simply served, it was always a delight to have her wait on us and spoil us just a little.

Yes, she was frugal and thrifty. She cut her paper napkins in half. The wax paper out of cereal boxes was neatly removed, folded, and put away for some future use. Tea bags were good for another cup of tea on the morrow. Leftovers were eaten, not discarded.

Both Mary and her husband Julius were generous in giving to the church, to missions and needy families. They loved giving surprise gifts. Every Christmas they gave a gift to nieces and nephews. Mary supplied her entire clan of relatives with pot holders. Every adult grandchild, married or single, has her colorful pot holders in their kitchen drawer. You will find them in North Carolina, Vermont, Colorado, Los Angeles, Fresno, Fowler, and Lodi, as well as Ontario, Manitoba, Alberta, Saskatchewan, and British Columbia!

Faithful in church attendance, busy in women's sewing circles, Mary cut many a square out of castoff clothing and made quilts for Mennonite Central Committee and World Concern. Dozens of her hand-tied quilts went overseas to needy and poverty-stricken countries.

When Mary was diagnosed with breast cancer, she accepted that burden stoically, as she accepted all problems and burdens in the many years of her life. When her strength failed her, she reluctantly closed her sewing machine and prayed for younger hands to continue the work that she could no longer do.

When she was close to death and in a coma, it was my great privilege and honor, along with my sister Elsie, to keep day and night vigil at her bedside. There was no sign of recognition or awareness until we sang to her the familiar "Amazing Grace."

> *Amazing grace, how sweet the sound*
> *That saved a wretch like me..*
> *I once was lost but now I'm found,*
> *Was blind but now I see.*

And also the old German song:
> *Gott ist die Liebe*
> *Lässt mich erlosen*
> *Gott ist die Liebe*
> *Er liebt auch mich*

It was then her eyelids fluttered briefly, and she uttered one word—"Singing."

Several days later, October 4, 1992, on a cloudy Sunday afternoon, a hush and stillness seemed to pervade the hospital room. Julius, Elsie, and I stood at Mary's bedside and watched her closely. She breathed lightly for awhile, then unevenly, and suddenly several long breaths. I counted to five and waited for the next breath, but she had passed from life to death in those few moments. Then Julius, Elsie, and I clung together and wept.

> *Mary, you've walked the narrow*
> *Path you chose,*
> *You've found release*

From all your woes.
Your suffering is gone and past,
And you're at home
In heaven at last.
Now, rest in peace.

IN the presence of all her siblings, many relatives, and friends, our dear sister was laid to rest. We mourn her departure and miss her so much. But we know she is now in the mansion God has prepared for her.

Good bye, Mary. We love you.

A Letter to Frank (1996)

Dear Frank,

I have been doing a lot of reminiscing the last few weeks about the time when we were young and carefree, making our own fun, living on the farm at Margaret, Manitoba.

I especially recall freezing cold winter nights when it seemed the whole world was covered in sparkling snow and the moonlight was almost as bright as day.

After our supper of fried potatoes and brown bread, which you loved so much, Mother allowed us to go and play in the snow. We tramped and romped, slid and tobogganed down the ravine behind our unpainted barn in that glittering snow. When our noses and hands were well nigh frozen and our bodies near the boiling point beneath the strange assortment of our clothing, we left our play reluctantly and were hungry again! Did we then eat head cheese with onions and brown bread? While Dad sipped his hot tea out of a glass or drank his coffee out of a saucer, and Mother sat patiently darning socks, the steel needle glinting in the soft light of the kerosene lamp as she skillfully wove the yarn over and under that big hole in the sock.

Remember the Sunday morning in the summer of 1936 when Dietrich and I woke up the whole family by singing "Der Tag Ist am Ersheinen" ("The Morning Light is Breaking") at our parents' window?

In October of that year, at our wedding you heroically recited that German poem that you still know word for word. How amazed I was when you recited that for me just two years ago!

Back to summers at the farm, when Mother sent us out to pick Saskatoons so she could make those delicious, thin pancakes with a handful of the berries on top—what a delightful treat that was for us.

I could go on and on, but I don't want to wear you out completely. But what great memories we have of that big, happy family of ours.

We never thought then how it would be when we would be parents or grandparents, did we? You now have a wonderful, caring family and grandchildren all living close by. Isn't that a blessing?

Now I must close and tell you that I love you and care

about you and pray you will receive strength for each day. God only gives us one day at a time with the promise that He will never leave us nor forsake us. Great is His faithfulness!

Because I love you—Anne

❋

A Tribute to Frank Warkentin
My brother who died of cancer on April 10, 1996

I picked a rose for you today
With fragrance sweet
And lovingly I placed it
At the Master's feet.

I tearfully recall
The years so long ago
When we were gathered
Round the lamplight glow.

And as this rose full-blown
Tender and strong
Has triumphed through
The winter storm

And summer warm

When life has taken of its due
The petals fade and fall
And return to God

The essence of its hue.
So God will pour
From heavens store
His Glory over you.

FIFTEEN

Dietrich

❋

This is Your Life, Dietrich Friesen
For his 70th Birthday—January 1984

Across the sea, 'mid ice and snow
In weather thirty-five below,
Siberia, we shout ahoy
Was birthed a little Friesen boy.

How happy was the family then.
Another boy 'mongst mostly men.
They could always use another hand
To work that cold relentless land.

Sickness of small pox and typhoid came.
Years of worry, labor, and shame.

Not enough food to put on the table.
'Twas more than to cope, the parents were able.

Then death knocked at the Friesen home
And took their father to heaven above.
How desolate then the family felt.
Could they survive this frigid belt?

This country had dealt them cruel blows.
The snowstorms came and they all but froze.
Winters were endless, summers too short.
They began a dream of a different sort.

The decision was made through prayers and tear;
They would move to a country they'd heard of for years.
So all of the property was finally sold
Which gave them some rubles and a little gold.

They made new ticking for their feather beds
In blue and gray and even reds.
They roasted the zwieback firm and brown
And packed them in baskets with rope tied around.

The pillowcases in snowy white
With inset lace and buttons bright.
Very few things could they bring along
On this fearful journey so far and long.

With doubts and trembling their mother took
Her sons, with never a backward look.
Would there be good fortune in this far away land,
With customs unknown, new language to understand?

Into cattle trains they were hastily sent;
Their hearts and minds with fears were rent.
Soon after they were on the heaving ocean
Deathly sick from the constant motion.

"Dear Father in Heav'n, do not us forsake
But safely to our home in Canada take."
They prayed, "Jesus Savior, pilot me
Over this life's tempestuous sea."

The family was met at a rural station
In this wonderful country, this new nation.
When friends took them in, oh, what rejoicing
And once more their happiness they were voicing.

They settled down and thanked their God
For bringing them onto this freedom sod.
Dietrich, the youngest, was the only one
Who could go to school, of all the sons.

But never a question could he ask;
No one understood him from desk to desk.

The boys all looked so tidy and neat
And he was a misfit from shorn head to feet.

He looked at his clothes and they weren't right.
The britches too short, the waistcoat too tight.
He couldn't read or spell or talk.
He couldn't wait from that school to walk.

But soon things began to fall into place.
Dietrich learned the problems to face.
He soon moved to the city and there he found
A new world of music, what glorious sound.

The best thing that happened in Dietrich's life
Was the day he met his future wife.
He heard her sing, he loved her voice
And promptly decided she was his choice.

They shared their love, their music, their song
And raised their family before too long.
Saturdays the opera on radio was aired,
For this all the children to list, prepared.

He directed choirs, taught people to sing,
Sang till he made the rafters ring.
All through the week and Sundays too
Services, broadcasts, and concerts to do.

Church work and college were first on the list,
Classes or services were rarely missed.
The students he taught were his delight
As he watched them doing things just right.

Manitoba, Kansas, California, too,
Oregon, Nebraska to name just a few.
These are places where we have wonderful friends,
A circle beloved that never ends.

Merciful, gracious, the Lord has blessed,
Exceeding abundant, more than we asked.
And now you have reached the big seven-oh,
Praise God from whom all blessings flow.

Curriculum Vitae of Dietrich Friesen

*D*ietrich's musical career began when he was elected director of the North Kildonan Male Chorus in 1939. In 1941 he was invited to conduct the Elmwood Mennonite Brethren Choir (then known as North End), a position that had previously been filled by Mr. Ben Horch. Dietrich held this position until his departure for the United States in 1950. In 1943, Dietrich assumed leadership of the Canadian Sunday School Mission Radio Choir, where he served until 1950. From 1945 to 1950, he instructed music in the

Winnipeg Bible Institute. In 1948, Dietrich also taught music in the Winkler Bible Institute for one year.

Dietrich's post-high-school studies in Canada consisted of private instruction in voice from Mr. Ben Horch, Stanley Hoban, Charles Milau, and W.H. Anderson, and the study of music theory with Dr. Niermeier. He enrolled in the Mennonite Brethren Bible College in Winnipeg in 1945 and completed the course leading to a diploma in sacred music, simultaneously completing an Associate of Arts in Music with the Royal Conservatory of Music in Toronto.

In the autumn of 1950, Dietrich entered Tabor College and completed requirements for his B.A. He took post-graduate work at the University of Wichita, from which he graduated in the summer of 1953 with a Master's degree in Music. While in Kansas, Dietrich conducted the First Baptist Church Choir in Durham and also taught music in the Durham High School for a year and several months.

The position of Music Director at Pacific College in Fresno was offered to Dietrich in 1952, and he headed that music department for fourteen years. He subsequently served as Assistant Professor of Music, teaching theory, conducting sight-singing, holding choir seminars, and instructing in private and class voice. He also conducted the Fresno Oratorio Society Chorus in two productions each year.

Additional post-graduate studies consisted of two summer courses at the University of Minnesota, where Dietrich studied under Robert Shaw and Dr. Julius Herreford—one summer in New York under Dr. Peter Wilhowsky, and one autumn quarter in Vienna, Austria, where he observed and studied with some of the most renowned vocal instructors and with the great musical lecturer, conductor, and recording artist Hans Sworowsky, of the Academy of Music and Performing Arts.

Since 1939 Dietrich has had the opportunity of conducting church choirs, mainly in the Mennonite Brethren churches. This consisted of ten years in Winnipeg, fourteen years in the Bethany Mennonite Brethren Church in Fresno, and several other choirs intermittently. It was his privilege to conduct choral clinics in British Columbia, Alberta, Manitoba (for some eight successive years), and Ontario in Canada, and Kansas, Washington, Oregon, and California in the United States.

Dietrich was chairman of the United States Mennonite Brethren Board of Church Music for nine years and served on various music committees in California for some time. He had a part in compiling and editing the first Mennonite Brethren hymnal for the Canadian Mennonite Brethren Conference in 1948-1950, and initiated the joint effort of compiling, editing, and publishing the present Mennonite Brethren hymnal for the United States and Canada.

Dietrich always believed it to be his distinct privilege, by choice, to serve the Mennonite Brethren Conference during his life. This was a service to which he would dedicate his remaining years until the Lord took him home.

Your Song

Your golden voice moves my heart.
Ever so gently it sings
As if fingers of velvet
Are softly touching the strings
Of muted harp.
The glow of that sweet song
Is like a flame
That's kindled by a meandering breeze
And oh, so swiftly now begins to burn
As your emotions upward turn.

My heart and soul respond in joyful ways
Ascendent sings the song
On silver waves.
It speaks of heights
Too glorious to bear
And only divine heaven can compare.

Oh song, so lovely was thy sound,
That in my vibrant heart
I'll keep thee bound
So cherish and with cords of love entwine
So that forever I will keep thee mine!

The Death of My Beloved
February 28, 1988
(Written one year later)

It is one year ago today that we laid our dear daddy, darling husband, and sweet Opa to rest. How we have all missed him and long to have him back—in a selfish sense. However, we know Dietrich is in a better place, no more sickness or sadness, in the presence of the Lord.

I remember that time as though it were yesterday. February 27, 1988, was a beautiful spring day in Fresno, just nice enough to make us forget winter's cold and dreary fog. The early blossoms decorated the otherwise bare branches of the fruit trees in the orchards, with their faces turned toward the sun, even as our hearts are turned toward hope. The sky had the promise of warmth and more beauty to follow.

Dietrich had been transferred to a convalescent hospital and was very ill. Eugene had arrived from Connecticut a few days earlier to be close to his father, and it was such a comfort to have him to lean and rely on both at home and at the hospital. The doctor could not predict how much longer Dietrich might endure, so we spent as much time as possible at his side.

On that Saturday morning, Eugene and I left early to spend the day with Dietrich. We talked to him, held his hands, sang, prayed, and played tapes of Eugene's compositions, not knowing whether he was aware of our presence.

As I watched Dietrich's face closely, I thought I saw a faint smile and believed he was hearing our beautiful music. Could it have been heaven's glorious music he heard beckoning him?

We tried in vain to give him water to drink, but there was no response. We wet his parched lips and continued to stroke his hands and face—with all the love we had for him, we could not bring him out of his sleep. So we watched and waited.

At five o'clock, Eugene and I prepared to leave the hospital and asked the nurse for her opinion about Dietrich's condition. She could not give us a definite answer. So we left with heavy hearts to join the rest of the family for dinner at Ed and Kathy's. Wally and Dolly were there, also Vic and Darlene, and Milt. Allan was on a business trip in New Mexico, so he would not arrive until Sunday.

After dinner, the boys decided that they would all go to the hospital to be with their father. Since I was physically exhausted and emotionally drained, the children encouraged me to stay home. With Ed and Kathy hovering over me, I was able to rest, knowing I was being cared for and that Dietrich was not alone.

At their father's bedside, the boys played a tape of the 500-voice male chorus that Dietrich had directed several years earlier. With their beautiful voices blending, they sang for him, staying at his side for several hours. Eugene was the first to leave, being concerned about my need for rest.

At nine o'clock, as Eugene and I were getting into the car to go home, there was a sudden gust of wind almost taking our breath away, bringing an unexpected change in the weather.

After driving a few blocks in the angry, howling wind with debris and papers blowing along the streets, we pulled up at a traffic light and noticed that everything behind us was pitch black, every light out. We continued on as branches, leaves, anything that was loose was being swirled about by the relentless wind. It was awesome.

At the next traffic light, while the wind continued its fury, again all the lights blacked out behind us, almost as if we had pulled a switch. Somehow the storm left me troubled. I didn't think of it then, but now, with hindsight, I wonder if the Lord was giving us a message.

As we drew closer to home, the wind abated and we arrived without mishap. Eugene and I visited briefly over a cup of tea and went to bed, weary in body and sad in heart. For some reason, Eugene decided to sleep on the living room couch. I was able to fall asleep soon after I went to bed. However at 5 AM I awoke from the most incredible dream.

In my dream, I was deathly ill, so ill that my mind and body were not able to be together. It was a sickness of such magnitude that the mind could not comprehend. My mind told me, "No, you cannot allow this illness in your body because you have to continue here for Dietrich and the family." But my body was ill beyond all help. And a sense of dreadful fear overwhelmed me. Then a verse came to me, and as I spoke it, a warm peace enveloped me.

"God has not given us the spirit of fear; but of power, and of love, and of a sound mind." –II Timothy 1:7

As I slept and dreamed, the hospital had called Kathy to inform the family of Dietrich's passing, which I would later realize coincided with the exact hour of my dream. Eugene awoke to the sounds of the children's arrival, and as they entered, I awoke from my dream, heard the squeak of the front door, and immediately knew I had gone through the throes of death with my beloved husband. I sat up on the edge of the bed. When the children reached my room, I said, "Daddy is gone!" I felt a wave of healing, as if a great burden had been lifted off my heart, while my tears watered that part of my heart that was left. Dietrich went to be with his Lord at the exact time of my dream (according to the death certificate) and I firmly believe that our spirits agonized together at that time.

As the children enveloped me in their arms, we shared a sense of comfort and love as we together experienced the pain and grief of our loss. It was a beautiful hug-in, and I received strength from the presence of my children, knowing they would uphold and help me through this time of sorrow.

It is a source of joy to me that Dietrich went to heaven on a Sunday, our most precious day of the week—Sunday, the day we would go to church to worship with fellow

Christians, sing songs of praise to our God whom we love and honor and who has dealt with us so wonderfully with mercy and grace.

*"How blessed is everyone who fears the Lord, who walks in His ways. When you shall eat of the fruit of your hands, you will be happy, and it will be well with you." (*Psalm 128:1-2)

Certainly I can say our Daddy was one who was happy in his work for the Lord, and he was blessed beyond measure here and will be rewarded in heaven.

The days that followed were busy ones, indeed. Our children and their spouses were all home, and it was wonderful the way they took care of everything that needed to be done. Jason and Samantha, Chris and Allan's two oldest, were the only grandchildren that were not able to come. It was a special and meaningful time for our entire family, sharing together our love and our grief for our departed loving husband and father.

The food brought by friends during those days was enough to feed all of us for the entire week. There was very little we had to buy. The beautiful flowers and cards from family and friends were overwhelming.

The comments from former students continue to be a source of encouragement. Dietrich is well remembered and loved. He touched the lives of countless young students with his ability to promote good sacred music. His impact is far-reaching, especially in our Mennonite Brethren churches.

Dietrich had planned what he wanted for his memorial service, which made it easier for us. He had chosen the people he wanted to officiate, as well as the music and musicians.

March 3, 1988, the day of the memorial service, was bright and sunny. The service was music-filled, meaningful, emotional, and uplifting—a praise service to our Lord.

The inscription on the headstone of Dietrich's grave reads:

"He put a new song in my mouth. Psalm 40:3"

What a blessing to know that a new song is now ringing in the courts of heaven!

To God be the Glory! Worthy is the Lamb! Hallelujah!

The finality of death is so hard to accept. After sharing over fifty-one years together in marriage, separation from Dietrich has been a difficult reality. But the Lord has been so gracious to me, and the promises of His Word are a source of comfort and solace, especially in times of tears and heartache.

"The eternal God is my refuge, and underneath are the everlasting arms." (Deuteronomy 33:27)

This Was Our Life

'Twas the year '36 and the month of October
When Anne Warkentin pledged her heart to her lover,

To Dietrich Friesen she gave her hand,
The biggest catch in all the land.

Tall, dark, and handsome, and extremely rich,
If not in money, he had perfect pitch.
The wedding was pompous and exceedingly long,
Three or four preachers tied a knot firm and strong.

Anne's fondest dream was to live in the city,
Away from the farm and its nitty gritty.
In a rattly old car to Winnipeg they went
There to live in an upstairs room for rent.

Happily they dwelt in the little room,
Apple boxes and orange crates stacked one on one,
This was their china closet, buffet and all,
Perfect contentment—be it ever so small.

The years flew by until one day
Dietrich decided he couldn't stay
Away from college anymore
And so he entered school's open door.

Higher learning was difficult,
Too late smart and too soon old.
But off they went to the USA
With their four children they were on their way.

To Tabor College in a little town
With one street up and one street down.
Dietrich studied, directed, and taught
And time just few with singing fraught.

A happy time in Kansas land,
Many joys with new found friend.
The call to Fresno changed all that.
They'd have yet another place to hang their hat.

While Annie was baking and cooking at home,
Cleaning and washing in billows of foam,
Dietrich was teaching the students to sing
And the rafters at Pacific now with music ring.

Choir practice, choir practice, that was their lot,
Early or late it was never forgot.
Summer and winter, spring time and fall,
Choir practice, choir practice one and all.

We all think Fresno can't be beat
In spite of its fog, its smog, and its heat.
For thirty-seven years this is home, sweet home
From this fair place we will not roam.

All through the years we have sought to serve
And from our duties we dared not swerve.

With joy and love our voices we raised
So may our God in heaven be praised!

*

A Letter to My Husband

O, my dear love,

My heart was so tragically shattered that Sunday morning when you left me for your heavenly home. I just cannot fit the problem parts together again. I want to tell you how very dearly I loved you from the time of our first meeting in October of 1934. It was love at first sight for both of us that evening in North Kildonan.

All the years we were married, our love was so strong, our hearts had come to fulfillment, and we believed they would remain entwined for always. So often you expressed the desire that we might depart from this world together, but that was not in the Lord's plan.

It is Sunday again—always our special day, and you are not here to share the joy of worship, singing, and praise with me. I can never again feel the exhilaration of the wonderful oratorios, anthems, and gospel songs that you so ably directed for thirty-eight years. What a blessing those years were for us.

On the rare Sunday afternoons that we had a few hours to ourselves, you took me by the hand and guided me to rest by tucking me under a warm blanket, telling me again how much you loved me, and bid me sleep until you came to wake me in your endearing way.

How I miss your wonderful bear hugs! They were total security. I heard today that a person needs three hugs every day. You gave me many more, and that must be why I miss you so much. As long as you were able, you told me of your constant, continual love. Your tender and gentle ways were my comfort, inspiration, and strength.

You never failed to praise me for my domestic ability. My baking and cooking were (in your words) "the best you've ever made." You were always willing to be my taster and sampler, and you enjoyed every bite.

When I listen (as I am right now) to music by Mendelssohn and Beethoven, I can still feel your hand reaching over to take my hand very firmly, as together we confirmed our enjoyment of the beautiful classical piece. Those times I cherish in my memory. They are a strong link in the golden chain of our happy years together.

I am aging rapidly—my step is becoming slower and not as sure as in days gone by. The sparkle in my eyes that you loved so much is no longer there. I do not mean to let this happen, but you are not here to kindle that flame, and so it has faded.

I'm glad I told you all those years that you were the best and most beloved husband and choir director, as well as father and soloist. I wish we had a count of all the weddings you sang for. You and I sang duets at many a wedding too, most frequently in Winnipeg. "Heilge Liebe" in Winnipeg and "Together with Jesus" in the USA. A blessed memory!

After a performance of an oratorio, we would sit for hours before we could unwind enough to go to sleep, always upholding each other in the closeness of our love. I am so happy that I could share in a small degree the work of music that meant so much in your life. How often I thanked the Heavenly Father for the privilege of serving Him and His people with the gift He so graciously bestowed on you.

These are but a few of the sweet thoughts and memories that waft back to me. I will keep them stored in the innermost recesses of my heart and mind.

And so, my dear heart, I have found the good Lord is my stronghold and fortress through all the grief and sorrow. I can believe and rely on His Word: *"For I, the Lord They God, will hold thy right hand, saying unto thee, 'Fear not; I will help Thee.'"* (Isaiah 41:13)

In the words of the duet by Henry Smart that we so often sang:

His goodness and mercy shall follow me still
While life's earnest duties I daily fulfill.
'Til joyous my spirit shall claim its reward
And dwell ever more in the house of the Lord.

Yea, though I walk through death's dark valley and shade
I will not by evil be ever dismayed.

The Lord is my shepherd
I never shall want!

You are now in the presence of our Savior and are be-holding His power and glory. And until the day God calls me home to join you in His heaven, I must bid you my fondest farewell—*aufwiedersehn.*

Your loving and devoted wife,

Anne

Dietrich Friesen: A Tribute
(1913-1988)

On the frozen steppes of Siberia where you were born, your father placed his work-worn hands on your head and pronounced a blessing on you—that you would become a teacher and prepare young people to serve with the gifts of music and song in the church and community.

Your introduction to choral directing came at an early age. Your elementary school teacher called on you unex-pectedly, thrust a baton into your hand, and ordered you to conduct your classmates in a favorite school song. You managed to do that quite naturally, both to your astonish-ment and your teacher's satisfaction.

The enjoyment of that experience gave birth to your desire to become a choral director and singer. The seed was sown, and it grew and flourished. You devoted your heart and mind to the furtherance of music education.

Of the many faces of music—oratorio, opera, classical

and sacred—you chose the music of the church as your life's vocation.

This evening, we, your family, colleagues, alumni, and friends, venerate your achievements, your faithfulness, and enthusiasm in your work at Fresno Pacific College and in the church, both in Canada and the United States. You dedicated your gifts to shaping and guiding thousands of voices. Many of those voices are here tonight to honor you and continue the work you began. As in Psalm 150, "Let us continue to praise the Lord with strings, voice and organ."

FPC Dietrich Friesen
Memorial Endowment Fundraiser
March 1990

For weeks I was filled with excitement—excitement that kept me awake at night thinking and scheming! I was awaiting the arrival of my sons. And when the children come home, a mother's thoughts turn to food, the boys' favorite food. Soon I was baking chocolate chip cookies, matrimonial cake, and sugar cookies. Tapioca pudding for Allan (his favorite). *Verenika, borscht* and *zwieback*. By unanimous vote there was one meal of Russian pancakes with sausage and boysenberry sauce.

Eugene was the first to arrive, with his trusty cello under one arm and his future wife Wendy at his side. We had a wonderful evening with many tender moments of remembering bygone days.

Allan flew in from Denver, and we all met him at the airport. Once again, the loving greetings and hugs took over. Kathy, Ed, and Vic joined us for *verenika* dinner that evening, and I was in my glory. What a joy to have loving children around me once again.

From then on, it was a whirlwind of activity. All the last minute details and rehearsals for the Friday evening concert at Pacific College. We were all involved in one way or another. Ed had made a double, eight-foot picture frame to display photos of Dietrich in the early years at the college. This was set up in the entrance of the banquet hall and decorated with miniature white lights, beautiful plants and flowers, even a little waterfall. There is a tremendous amount of planning and a lot of hard work involved to make dinner for four hundred people a success. We only did a small part of it. The college did the biggest part.

Suddenly it was Friday afternoon, time to get dressed and go to the party. Walt and Dolly, Randy and Rick arrived and we all made our way to the college special events center.

We were greeted by the brass band playing out in front of the building. People were streaming in, so many dear friends, everyone in a festive, happy mood with loving greetings and hugs.

The banquet hall looked magnificent. Round tables

with white linen cloths and wine-colored napkins. The centerpiece on every table was a mirror square with three votive candles, decorated with a narrow, wine-colored ribbon and bows. The whole scene looked like a fairyland.

Hors d'oeuvres were served at six o'clock, and we all had a good chance to meet people and chat.

Dinner was catered by one of Fresno's hotels. Chicken breasts with lemon sauce, pilaf and green beans, preceded by green salad and coffee, sparkling apple cider, and rolls. Dessert was strawberry shortcake.

The concert was unspeakably beautiful. Eugene can truly make the cello speak and sing, laugh and cry. He has a marvelous, God-given gift. Paul Halley from New York accompanied him. Milton directed the combined choir, college and alumni, in one of Dietrich's favorite anthems, "How Lovely is Thy Dwelling Place" by Brahms. I wept through most of the concert, my heart overflowing with love and gratitude for all the wonderful years with Dietrich and now carried on by our children.

The concert was well received. The musicians received a standing ovation and had to play encores. So many of the people expressed their appreciation for the work Dietrich did. Now that work with be continued by others who will receive help from his scholarship.

The entire evening was a wonderful tribute to Dietrich. He has not been forgotten. Many of my friends told me they thought that Dietrich had heard all this, and many of them said they wished he had been there to enjoy it.

As all good things must end, this concert ended in much applause. We were all happily exhausted, and it took hours for us to unwind. Now the Dietrich Friesen Benefit Concert is history.

Saturday morning, we were all invited to Vic and Darlene's. There, we relaxed and enjoyed each other. Vic barbecued chicken and made coleslaw. Darlene had baked *zwieback* and some of us had brought dessert. It was a fun evening, and some of us (including me) enjoyed a session in the hot tub.

Sunday evening, we said goodbye to Gene and Wendy. They had announced their engagement on Saturday night. On Monday, it was Allan's turn to leave. And now my rooms are tidy and empty again. Needless to say, the crying towel was much in evidence, as life and time goes on.

This gives you an idea of the activities and excitement we had during the time from March 20 to 26. I am grateful for this event.

Tribute to Dietrich Friesen
By Dr. Larry Warkentin

On January 11, 1914, a baby boy was born in Russia, and on February 28, 1988, 74 years later, a much-loved man was laid to rest in Fresno, California. Between those two dates, Dietrich Friesen fulfilled his destiny as a music minister.

Music was not something he chose to do—it was

something that chose him. It was not something he studied and performed; rather, it was something that sprang from within him. Even the woman he married was chosen by music. I have heard him tell the story of how he heard a beautiful voice singing in a church choir—and he married the best soprano in the choir! For him, Anne was more than a voice. She was a faithful wife, a devoted companion, a loving mother of their six children, a strong support during his years of declining health, and an unselfish hostess.

Dietrich Friesen was not the first music teacher at Pacific Bible Institute, but he was the first one to make a major impact on its music program. He came to PBI in August of 1952, when the school was only seven years old, and taught that year for the grand sum of $3,500.

Dietrich had earned a music certificate from Mennonite Brethren Bible College in Winnipeg, a Bachelor of Arts in music from Tabor College, and a Master of Arts, with vocal emphasis, at Wichita University, Kansas.

He conducted his first choir in the North Kildonan Mennonite Brethren Church in 1939, and he continued to conduct at Fresno Pacific College and in the Fresno area churches until the 1970s.

He taught many subjects while at FPC, including music history and music theory, but his greatest contribution was in voice and choir instruction.

He had a wonderfully warm baritone voice. I remember

providing piano accompaniment for him as he sang "O, Du Mein Holder Abendstern," by Wagner. There was a pure quality to his voice which was God-given. No amount of training could have created such a voice. It was a gift. He was also gifted as a vocal teacher. He was able to inspire and enrich each vocal student that came to him.

When I joined the music department in 1962, Dietrich had built the choral program into a highly respected tradition. With the choir, he toured annually into Canada, the Pacific Northwest, and the Midwest. During those first years, the choir was large and the college enrollment was small, so when the choir went on tour, school was closed.

My office was next door to the choir rehearsal room, and I have distinct memories from those days. One memory is the beautiful sound that came from his choir, and the other is the frequency of laughter from the group. Dietrich had a quiet, dry sense of humor, and students responded to it enthusiastically.

One of Dietrich's great loves was conducting large mass choirs. He was instrumental in organizing the Fresno Oratorio Society. This organization combined the college choir with a large number of singers from the Fresno churches. For several years, they performed *The Messiah* in larger churches, and several years in the Convention Center Theater. In the spring of each year, Dietrich would select another of the great oratorios for presentation. *Elijah, The Creation, German Requiem, Choral Fantasy*, and Faure's

Requiem were some of the works he loved and performed. In rehearsal, he would work unrelentingly for the style and tone he sensed should be there. In performance, he worked with such intensity that his clothes would be soaking wet from perspiration.

Conducting is an invisible art. The conductor is a facilitator. He sets the tempo, indicates the interpretation, and establishes the style. So, we ask, what remains of Dietrich's work? Is it invisible? What monument remains?

The answer is similar to that written of Sir Christopher Wren, the English architect. In the great St. Paul's Cathedral in London, designed by Wren, is the simple epitaph, "If you would see his monument, look around you."

As we look around us, we see a loving family. We see a college that continues to value choral music. We see conductors, such as Roy Klassen, who were his students. We see singers, such as Ed Willems, who carry on his vocal legacy. We see churches that are still using the hymnal that he helped to create and promote. Those of us who worked with him carry memories of his gentle determination, his vision for beautiful music, and his devotion to the calling given to him by God. These are his monuments. On that monument let us write these words from the writing of St. Paul: "He has fought the good fight, he has finished the race, he has kept the faith."

SIXTEEN

Grandchildren

*W*hat a blessing and joy my children, grandchildren, and great-grandchildren add to my life.

I only recall my Grandmother Warkentin from Russia vaguely. She stayed with us sporadically and was very old. I was in awe of her, though I did not feel close to her. I missed that and hoped that when the time came for my own grandchildren, I would be able to have a close relationship with them.

In January 1960, our first granddaughter was born. What a family celebration that turned out to be! As the years went on, three grandsons were born. We rejoiced for all of them and had wonderful times together. Those four cousins grew up to be very close, and it was many years before the next batch of grandchildren came along.

The grandchildren and great-grandchildren have provided so much fun for our family. We have had *zwieback* and cookie-making lessons until the dough turned gray—but always with lots of love involved. They have entertained with dress-up plays and skits and have sung and played concerts. I have been the wicked witch, the queen, or the scullery maid for them when we played Cinderella. I have played "Blind Man's Bluff," running around blindly until my shins were black and blue. I have hidden in musty closets for Hide and Seek. To be a good sport, I even took a ride on the roller coaster at Santa Cruz—I considered it to be a great chiropractic treatment!

Now some of the grandchildren are husbands, wives, and parents themselves, and I couldn't love them more! They treat me with great respect and as their best friend. I love to cook and bake their favorite "Grandma" foods and baby-sit the little ones. I am always so proud and happy when the grown grandchildren and great-grandchildren greet me with a warm hug and when the little ones come running into my arms with hugs and kisses. What could be more rewarding for a grandmother and great-grandmother!

This is the prayer I pray for all of them:

Dear Jesus, You know how much I love each one of these children. But I know You love them much more than I do. I gather them all together in a circle and I ask You to be the center of that circle. Touch each one with Your love, Your grace and Your tender mercies. Amen.

KATHY's daughter, Diana, was our first grandchild. She is married to Kevin Douglass and they have three children, Justin, Branden, and Marissa. Marissa was born three years after Diana suffered a bout of ovarian cancer. They live in Fresno, California, where Kevin works for SaveMart Super Market and Diana works part-time at Community Hospital.

Brian is Kathy's son. He is married to Sheri, and they also live in Fresno, California, where they are involved in the music at Bethany Mennonite Brethren Church. They both work at Valley Children's Hospital, Brian in pathology and Sheri as manager in the lab. They have two daughters, Emily and Chelsea.

Randall is Wally and Dolly's oldest son. He lives in Los Angeles and is a graphic artist who designs and produces books and magazines. Randall has loved books from early childhood and is responsible for putting this writing into book form. He has been a great encourager to me in the years it took for me to write this story.

Rick is Wally and Dolly's youngest son and is married to Bunni Magison. They reside in Fresno, California. Rick was in a skiing accident in 1984, but has experienced a remarkable recovery for which we are so thankful. And yes, he still skis! Rick works in sales for Sports Academy in Sanger, and Bunni is a graphic designer for the San Joaquin County Air Pollution Control District. They are involved with Sunday school and choir at the First Presbyterian Church.

Peter is Vic's adopted son. Vic, Darlene, and Peter are a completely happy family. Peter lives in San Jose, California, and works in computer technology.

Allan and Christine live in North Highlands, Colorado, and have two children, Jason and Samantha, from Christine's previous marriage. Both Jason and Samantha live and work in the Denver area. Chris and Allan together have two school-aged children, Sara and Addison. Sara has sung with the Colorado Children's Choir and also plays the piano. Addison is into baseball these days.

Anna and Zoe are Eugene's daughter from a previous marriage. Anna attends school and lives with Eugene and Wendy in Townshend, Vermont. Zoe lives in Alaska with her mother. Eugene and Wendy have two young children together, Noel and Mary.

Milton and Bendta have three young children. Analiese is Milton's daughter from a previous marriage, Evan is Bendta's son from a previous marriage, and together they have a son, Carsten.

A Wish

If I had the means,
I would give you wealth.

If I had the power,
I would give you health.

But all I have
Is a fervent prayer:

That God will bless you
Everywhere.

SEVENTEEN

Christmas

Things to Remember

$\mathcal{T}$he thrill of Christmas. The hope of Christmas. I have a wonderful warm feeling deep inside of me that cannot be quenched. Love and expectancy overrule all other feelings because it's in the air, all-permeating and delicious.

Expectancy is in the sparkle and glitter of the newly-fallen snow, reflecting the reds and greens of the shimmering lights, creating illusionary fantasies. I remember shopping at the elegant Hudson Bay Department Store in Winnipeg, and then hurrying to the streetcar in the snow. The wonderful security of my gloved fingers tucked in Dietrich's warm, strong hand, always guiding me so lovingly over the difficult places, always encouraging and supportive. Together we could make a memorable Christmas.

Wait. Wait! Only fifteen more days until Christmas. The excitement of it all almost made our hearts burst with happiness and anticipation.

Christmas Remembered

I remember baking days, creating marvels and wonders out of flour, sugar, butter, and eggs. There were hours of mixing and shaping, rolling and baking, and always each step was filled with love and care. The whole house was filled with the aroma of holiday spices. We felt enjoyment in giving to friends and neighbors, but there was always a bounty to save and sample while they were warm. How can any heart forget the pleasure of this day?

I have memories of times when the tree just wouldn't stand straight, and after and few anxious moments, we wired it to the wall! After the lights and ornaments were on, we thought it was the most beautiful tree ever. Even the artificial tree made a gorgeous Christmas spectacle with added lights, plenty of tinsel, and a new ornament or two. I remember when we lived on Fedora Street we used blue lights, blue and gold balls, and blue tassels.

In 1986, when Gene, Nora, Anna James, and Zoe Rose came for Christmas, we had a live tree with multi-colored lights, and I made sequin ornaments. What a joy to decorate that tree and enjoy the aliveness of it. To see the children's and grandchildren's eyes light up was reward enough. To have all the children home for Christmas is the ultimate fulfillment.

I remember the famous red tablecloth that has withstood all the years of spills of turkey gravy, cranberry sauce, fruit punch, and candle wax on Christmas Day, to say nothing of Christmas Eve's potato salad, *katletin*, cherry *mouss, zwieback*, braids, and cookies. The cloth has all of our children's, grandchildren's, and great-grandchildren's names embroidered on it, as well as the many friends and relatives that visited us over the years. It is a beloved keepsake. The names appear in every color of the rainbow, and we recall the joy the impact all these people have made on our lives. May this cloth go down in history and family heritage as a symbol of my life for all of you and for the many blessed Christmases to come.

The angel with her tarnished halo and gold foil wings visibly crumpled by now from years of flying is still clinging to the battered, shiny bouquet nestled in her scrawny, pipe-cleaner arms. She has given me such cheer each Christmas and must have a special place where the brilliantly-colored lights will reflect upon her wings and where her unseeing eyes can stare into the gaily decorated living room.

A newer arrival is the wooden deer whose red thumbtack eyes and plywood antlers can never harm or help man or beast. He holds his small head high, as if to the wind, looking and listening for any foe. With not a twitch of his handmade rope tail, he never objects to the endless variety of decoration or lights that I arrange on his rigid back. How could we do without his faithful vigil of all?

Every Christmas, as I struggle to drape the obstinate and resistant green plastic garland with the red poinsettias around the mirrored shelf in the living room and try to hide a string of lights in its stubborn vine, I threaten to dispose of it. Yet after every flower and light is in place, it has such a pleasant effect that I lovingly pack it away with the other Christmas treasure at the end of the season.

Epilogue: The obstinate plastic garland was stolen from my carport shortly after this writing. I still miss it!

THE music of Christmas, with its months of preparation and hours of rehearsing, was not to be compared with any other. Finally, the concert date arrived with the last minute details to plan. Every singer was filled with apprehension and excitement. The choir was in place, with the women dressed in long-sleeved white blouses and black skirts and the men in white shirts and dark suits.

Dietrich, resplendent in wing collar and butterfly white tie, with a smile in his blue eyes, lifted his baton, and glorious song filled the sanctuary. Hearts and voices are filled with praise of God's majesty as our very beings poured out in love for His Divine Lordship. Dietrich was always able to inspire each singer to do the very best possible. The audience sat hushed and enthralled, and the joy and hope of Christmas was visible in their faces. The music cleansed our hearts and souls and gave us rewards beyond compare.

Christmas is caroling. The first time for us was on a cold, snow-brightened night in the wide expanse of Marion County, Kansas. There was bright moonlight and frosty air, warm loving people, and chili, hot chocolate, and cookies. In later years we would go with our children and more recently with children and grandchildren. In fog or in mist, it was always such fun and a blessing. Lighting our candles out on the lawn, we lifted our voices into the dark night with a feeling of reverence and awe for the magical gift to mankind. We feel a kinship with each other that binds us together now and will keep us bound in love for future generations. God bless all carolers!

Christmas in Connecticut

It's Monday, December 28, and our destination today is fabulous New York City landmark, Radio City Music Hall, where we have tickets for a show entitled "Christmas Spectacular." Eugene and Zoe will stay home, while Nora, Anna James, and I plan to meet Nora's half-brother, his wife, and daughter at the hall. The drive to New York is uneventful—Nora is an excellent driver.

We arrive at the theater, along with thousands of people all in a holiday mood. Two grand organs are responding to the touch of two men in evening dress playing the wonderful carols we all know so well. I am overwhelmed by the magnificent sound and am compelled to sing as we are guided to our seats, which are in the very front row. Never has "O Come All Ye Faithful" been so meaningful for me.

As the spectacular begins, an orchestra accompanies a bevy of singers dressed in Victorian costume, blending their voices in beautiful harmony to excerpts from *Nutcracker Ballet, Scrooge* and *Santa's Toy Shop.* "The Dance of the Wooden Soldiers" is delightful, with forty ladies dressed in white soldier uniforms, walking without bending their knees or arms, all to music and in perfect formation. Santa is in his sleigh being pulled through the air by the flying reindeer. It is breathtaking, magnificently beautiful, and unbelievably marvelous. The grand finale is a scene of the Nativity, complete with Mary, Joseph, and the baby with their donkey, shepherds with the sheep, the three Kings on camels, all live and so close to us we need but put out our hands to touch them, As the two organs and the orchestra swell to a climax, I laugh, I sing, I cry as though my heart will break, all at the same time, the tears flowing down my cheeks. What a wondrous Christmas gift!

"Glory to God in the Highest; And on earth, peace and goodwill toward men!"

❋

Holiday Amaryllis

The full-blown beauty of crimson on my festive table
Brings renewal of the Christmas spirit

In the cold of December.
Beneath the three blossoms, another swelling bud
Struggling to give birth.
Four delicate green leaves curve gently,
Enhancing the magnificent blooms.

It began in a brown bulb planted in a man-made vessel
From which sprang this miracle of God!
A reminder of the Gift born in a lowly stable,
Under the star in Bethlehem

Christmas Eve in Winnipeg

If I could put the feeling into words
The softest snow, all feathery and white
The children's faces glow with sheer delight
There is no joy can quite compare
To Christmas in the sparkling air.

Each branch and bough festooned this night
With myriad of crystal flakes
Resembling choicest frosted cakes
Our footsteps crunching in the snow
As onward to the church we go

Children's voices lilting happy songs
Of Jesus in a manger—far away

Cradled warm on fragrant hay
Of little drummer boy, of lambs and sheep
The infant baby sweet—asleep.

Such memories my heart cannot forget
Though change has come as silent as the snow
And taken us along in gentle flow
When Christmas comes, with candles burning bright
I hear the children singing in the night.

Christmas Joy

Christmas is inside of me
The lights, the joy, the festive tree
It makes my step so feather light
My eyes a-twinkle starry bright!

I cherish each delightful card
Festooned on ribbon by the yard
With message of the newborn King
That makes the courts of Heaven ring.

How then can I so merry be?
When sorrow and sadness round I see
The Christ child came to dwell within
He took the fear and dread of sin.

The happiness that fills my soul
Measured would reach from pole to pole
A gift wrapped up and filled with glee
'Cause Christmas is inside of me!

'Twas the Night Before Christmas
(At our house, 1976—written in love, 1978)

The children from Lodi arrived Christmas Eve.
Grandpa and Grandma were dressed to receive.
Gram in her bright red Christmas best,
Gramps in his light gray suit and vest.

The supper was laid in traditional style,
With meatballs and zwieback and braids by the mile,
Cherry mouss, potato salad and cookies galore,
And no one was asking for anything more.

Then on to the church to hear music and singing
And always the church bells so joyously ringing,
To hear once again the "O Holy Night"
With faces beside me all happy and bright
Makes Christmas the most wonderful time of the year.
Thank you, Lord Jesus, for coming down here!

Now home to the tree and the gifts—what a pleasure

To open them all and each find a treasure.

'Twas the evening of Christmas and all through their home
Grandpa and Grandma did lonesomely roam.
The carpets were covered with boxes and papers
To remind us of children's most happy capers.
The table was strewn with crumbs from the food
That had tasted delightful, deliciously good.

The dishes in the kitchen were stacked so high,
But Grandpa and Grandma heaved not a sigh.
They tackled the crystal, the silver and plates
And didn't consider the leftovers' fates.

They thought about Christmases before and after
And remembered only the joy and the laughter.
They thought about children so loving and kind
And whispered a prayer—"God keep each one in mind."

So this is the way I'd like you all to remember
That wonderful Christmas day every December,
With parents and cousins and sisters and brothers
And always leave room in your hearts for others.

✿

Twelve Days of Christmas

On the first day of Christmas
I felt a little glum
There was so much work to be done.

On the second day of Christmas
I started on my list
And not a single name had I missed.

On the third day of Christmas
I worked from morn to night
And soon the house looked cheerful and bright.

On the fourth day of Christmas
I mixed cookie dough
And baked them all warmly—just so.

On the fifth day of Christmas
I had a little glow
One package came!

On the sixth day of Christmas
I sang a happy song
And the day didn't seem at all long.

On the seventh day of Christmas
The greetings had arrived
And my spirits were once again revived.

On the eighth day of Christmas
The sounds of music came
And glorified my dear Savior's name.

On the ninth day of Christmas
I wrapped the gifts with glee
And placed them by the Christmas tree.

On the tenth day of Christmas
I didn't have a care
For with others I my love could share.

On the eleventh day of Christmas
My soul was filled with cheer
For tomorrow Jesus Christ would be here.

On the twelfth day of Christmas
My heart o'er flowed with love
For the Glory came down from above!

❋

*

What is Christmas?

Carols sung on a moonlit night
In country where the snow lay bright;
Voices blending, joy unending,
Miracle of Christ's birth defending

Starlight gleaming on our way,
Gladness in our hearts today;
The babe of Bethlehem filled with awe,
Cradled in the sheltering straw.

The night is still and white with cold
While we proclaim the news of old,
"Christ is born!" Our lord is He,
Long has the world awaited Thee.

"O holy night," our voices sing
"All glory to our newborn King."
We hail Thee, Savior, Prince of Peace,
While the night is wrapped in snowy fleece.

O Christ of Christmas, be our guide
And keep us always by Thy side,
Our hearts and souls do now rejoice,
We give Thee homage with one voice.

*

Christmas Pleasures

The air all sweet
With sugar and spice,
The house is neat
With everything nice.

The ornaments glisten
In bright red and green,
And I can listen
To sounds unseen.

Sleigh bells ringing,
Sparkling snow,
Carolers singing,
Faces aglow.

Christmas abounding,
Joy fills our hearts.
Music resounding,
Sorrow departs.

Advent Song

Hazy twilight creeps easily
On the silent, gray street,
Lurks tranquil in the shadows
Of houses, barns,
And November foliage.
The branches are bare now,
Their leaves making beds of autumn
On the frigid earth,
Awaiting the blanket
Of feathers—light snow,
Creating a tinge of sadness
And longing, indefinable.
The heart yearns
For understanding and promise.

The promise of winter
With cold, crisp days
And the blinding whiteness
Of sparkling, shimmering snow,
The long, dark nights
With the scintillating radiance
Of myriads of stars.
And suddenly in December

One special Star!
The star of Bethlehem
Heralding the birth of Christ,
The light of the world,
Filling our hearts
With infinite joy and love.

*

Christmas Poem

Listen
To the bells
The chimes
They're ringing in
The steeple
I hear them in the wind
Wafted on the breeze
Through the trees

O'er the seas
Telling the story
And the glory
Of the Holy child
With mother mild
In the silent night
Of Christmas

Bringing joyful
Celebration
To every
Nation
Let your heart
Be filled with gladness
Banish all the thoughts
Of sadness
For on this day
Our Savior came
Now let us

Laud His Name!

EIGHTEEN

Special Memories

A Letter to My Friend Helen
August 29, 1990

*M*eine liebe Helene,

Here is your long absent friend—finally returned from my summer wanderings. First to the north and then to the east. All during my travels, I felt a strong, warm tug in my heart toward home and you—only to realize that your home is now in glory!

My dear Helen, there is a dread, a sadness, and sorrow in my heart when I think you will not be here for your birthday on September the fourth.

Never during the many happy years of our wonderful friendship did the thought of a parting by death occur to me. We were going to be friends forever. We were so young (at heart), full of hope, plans, and dreams of good times in our future.

We wanted to go to Hawaii again and recapture the fun of eating ice cream and pineapples and enjoying the deliciously exotic food from the Holiday Inn buffet so bountifully decorated with fragrant and exquisite orchids.

I want to send you beautiful, meaningful cards and poems, as I so often did. I have kept all the cards you sent me—they are my mementos. Two years ago, I sent you a green tobacco leaf from North Caroline for your birthday, and you laughed and laughed about that. You always appreciated a joke. You displayed genuine pleasure and joy from any favor or anecdote, and always, always that ready laugh!

Our telephone conversations were endless—and very often hilariously funny. Many times, even now, I need to call you to fill the void in my heart.

Oh, we had sorrows and heartache in common, too. After your husband Carl passed away, I was there for you. And when I lost Dietrich many years later, you helped me. We cried together and we prayed together and shared concerns for our children and their needs.

Many times, I wept when I saw you in your wheelchair. You could no longer walk or stand at will—it grieved me so. But you kept such a sweet, happy spirit.

We sang side by side in the Oratorio Choir—what a joy that was for both of us. We dressed in our lovely evening gowns (often the same color) and we were like the Bobbsey Twins—almost inseparable.

Now there is a valley between us through which I cannot walk. I must be content to cherish my memories of you.

This writing will be included in my memoirs, even as my poem is included in your life story.

I thank the Lord for the wonderful years we shared—you were always a source of joy and inspiration to me.

From this sad heart, farewell, my dearest friend. I will always miss you!

With love, Anne

＊

True Friendship
In memory of my beloved Friend Helen Maier Flaming

As the beauty of a full-blown rose
Began with a tiny bud,
So our friendship was born.
The rose is nurtured by
the warm caressing touch
of the sun;
the gentle refreshing rain,
and the sparkling dew.

Our friendship was nurtured
by smiles for its comfort,
by tears for its nourishment,

and by hugs for its strength
and durability.

Until it rang forth
in radiant beauty
and sweet fragrance.
Now is our love full blown
To keep and to cherish
even in parting
For me, friendship and roses
represent love.

Learning to Drive at Sixty-Five

Am I positively certain of what I see?
Is this phantom behind the wheel really me?
According to the way I feel,
I'm overwhelmed by this hunk of steel.

They told me, "Just learn to drive the car
So you can drive to the store, and not very far."
They promised, "So you can drive in a pinch."
They conned me into this, that's a cinch!

I hold the key in my shaky old hand,
The logic of cars I don't understand,

With hand and foot, with heart and mind,
I struggle to maneuver its unyielding kind.

I clutch the wheel most fervently.
I glance in the mirror and, lo, I see
A truck and trailer barreling oh so near,
My entire body's petrified with fear.

My heart beats louder than I've ever heard,
I scarcely comprehend the instructor's word.
One of those pedals on the floor
Has something to do with less or more.

The car comes to a screeching halt.
Student and teacher almost vault
Into that great big window pane.
Oh—I'll never, never do that again!

Cars coming at me from every side,
Whoever invented this crazy ride?
A horse and buggy, safe and slow,
That was the way we used to go.

I want to turn left when the light is green,
But suddenly and certainly unforeseen
Some character thinks he has right of way,
And I see stars—in the light of day!

I see them now on the mourner's bench
With flowing tears they cannot quench.
If Mom hadn't tried at sixty-five
Maybe today she'd be well and alive!

If only I'd learned at sweet sixteen
How painless and easy that would have been,
But now it's because of consequence
And at sixty-five—it's an awful chance.

Well, the day has come for the driver's test,
All night long I find no rest.
Green is for "Go" and "Stop" is red,
I've forgotten all else the instructor said!

My mouth is as dry as the desert sand,
But in my gnarled old wrinkled hand
I hold a little certificate
That proves: For some things it's never too late.

Now I'm so happy I learned to drive
When I was only sixty-five!

*

All About Birthdays (March 18, 1991)

Here I am one day into my 74th year and I can truthfully say, "I never felt better!" What wonderful gifts—life and health.

I have been doing a lot of reminiscing these past weeks, wondering what my parental home was like at the time of my birth. Was I born in the house that I remember before we left Russia on our move to Canada? The house with the "big room" where our parents' bed stood, piled high with snow white comforters and big, square, goose-down pillows with inset lace cases with handmade button holes and covered buttons?

I cannot recall that our birthdays were observed or even acknowledged. How different things are today, and how customs have changed. We have strayed so far from our roots. Not one of us could have dreamed our family would be scattered all over the North American continent.

My first birthday party was the year I turned 18. I was working in Winnipeg at the time and engaged to Dietrich. He arranged a surprise Sunday *faspa* in honor of my birthday and invited several of my girlfriends and my sister Helen.

On the menu were *zwieback*, jam, homemade dill pickles—deliciously tart and crisp—and sliced bologna. The big surprise was a bowl of Jell-O! To my great delight, it was bright red, sparkling, and wiggly Jell-O! This was an exceptional treat during the bleak times of the early

1930s. Dietrich's gift to me was a brown silk scarf with a yellow, green, and white design, which went well with the new brown coat I had bought with my own hard earned money—a fur-trimmed coat! I really felt like a queen that day. I still have the card Dietrich gave me, now a treasured souvenir.

I wore a pale blue taffeta dress my mother had made for me, and because there wasn't enough of the blue taffeta, she made the sleeves out of white fabric. This was devastating to my sense of fashion!

In our early years in Winnipeg, I sometimes invited my lady friends (other young mothers like me) for afternoon tea on my birthday. I went through a flurry of cleaning, polishing, and baking beforehand—my favorite meat-filled *pereshki*, the now famous Sugar Plum Braids, and butter tarts. I have always loved to entertain. Even though we had so little in those days, I was happy with what I could do. I was still using the beautifully embroidered tea cloths made out of Red Rose flour sacks that had been scrubbed and bleached. Now they were starched and ironed and looked pretty with my collection of china tea cups. The memory of that time brings warmth to my heart with love and a longing for the dear friends of long ago.

Since then, I have had birthday celebrations of all types. My children and grandchildren always make a big event of my birthday; they all know how much I love parties!

Several times, Kathy and Diana have taken me to

Pismo Beach or Santa Cruz on the California coast. We stay at a beautiful inn and do fun things like eat cookies in bed and stay awake half the night giggling and talking. When morning comes to our window stealthily, the darkness reluctantly turns opaque while dawn's filmy garments, scented with the early mists of the ocean, flutter mysteriously, drawing us out of a dream-filled night to a new day—a day to see the sun turn the foam on the ocean waves into wide strands of silver, borne onward until it changes into a thin, shimmering line that fades into the half circle of the sandy shore. After doughnuts and coffee, we run barefoot on the beach and jump into the hot tub.

For my 60th birthday, Dietrich arranged a party in grand style at the Hilton in downtown Fresno. Fresh flowers on the white linen-covered table, dear friends, and delectable food. Dietrich's gift to me that anniversary was a crystal necklace, which I wore on our 50th wedding anniversary.

This year's birthday was a week-long round of breakfasts, lunches, and dinners. After dinner at Diana and Kevin's, Kathy and Ed took me to their place where I spend the night in their pink guest room. Sunday to church and afterward to a lovely luncheon with dear friends. The grand finale was a concert by the Fresno Philharmonic Orchestra.

So for a lifetime of happy, healthy birthdays, I say, "The Lord hath done great things for me, whereof I am glad."

Birthday

A birthday is such a fleeting thing,
It's like a bird on swiftest wing,
Above the clouds it soars on high
'Mid sun and stars and blue of sky.

You dream your dreams on this fair day
And hope they're here fore e'er to stay.
So pleasant is this world of dreams
They'll never change, or so it seems.

But tomorrow comes and you're back down,
Your smile is gone—you wear a frown.
That birthday added on a year
As you wipe off that wistful tear.

But then, just think how you are blest,
More than you ever thought or asked.
Each day's a gift from God above,
So thank and praise Him for such love.

Maundy Thursday, or Holy Thursday
April 16, 1987 at Butler Church

A rugged cross is before us, the symbol of Christ's death; one banner on either side of the cross. One reads: "He died for us." The other reads: "He rose for us." The sanctuary is dim, the lights are low. Two tables covered with white linen, holding two white candles, the cup, and the bread.

Before we take the cup and the bread, we bow before Him in confession.

"We confess to you, Lord, what we are: we are not the people we like others to think we are; we are afraid to admit even to ourselves what lies in the depths of our souls. But we do not want to hide our true selves from you. We believe that you know us as we are, and yet you love us. Help us not to shrink from self-knowledge; teach us to respect ourselves for your sake; give us the courage to put our trust in your guidance and power.

"We also confess to you, Lord, the unrest of the world, to which we contribute and in which we share. Forgive us that so many of us are indifferent to the needs of our fellowmen.

"Forgive our reliance on weapons of terror, our discrimination against people of different races, and our preoccupation with material standards. And forgive us Christians for being so unsure of our good news and so unready to tell it.

"Raise us out of the paralysis of guilt into the freedom

and energy of forgiven people. And for those who, through long habit, find forgiveness hard to accept, we ask you to break their bondage and set them free, through Jesus Christ our Lord. Amen."

My heart is filled to overflowing with love and gratitude for such a Savior. We sing:

And can it be that I should gain
An interest in the Savior's blood?
Died He for me, who caused His pain,
For me who Him to death pursued.
Amazing love! How can it be
That Thou, my God, shouldst die for me?

For me to be reminded anew that my sins have been washed away, forgiven and forgotten, causes me to rejoice and be glad and praise the Lord for His great faithfulness.

We go to the communion table in groups of eight or ten. We each break off a piece of the bread and then partake together. "This is my body, broken for you."

We take the individual cups and again partake together. "In remembrance of me."

In the seventy years of my life, I had never experienced a foot washing. Jesus washed his disciples' feet just before the Passover Feast.

It was humbling and meaningful to have a dear friend of mine kneel before me and pour water over my feet and then dry them with a large towel. Such a wonderful love welled up in my heart. My eyes filled with tears. We hugged each other and felt so blest. Then I, in turn, knelt and washed her feet, and again was overcome with a deep sense of Christian love. We were thoroughly blessed. Jesus must have felt such a blessing when the woman anointed His feet with the expensive perfume.

We had a time for quiet meditation, and I was uplifted and strengthened, although my heart was grieved that my dear husband Dietrich could not be there to share in this wonderful experience and renewal of faith. The Lord has promised in His Word that He will never leave us nor forsake us.

So we celebrated Jesus' death and resurrection. Every Easter is a new beginning, and again we will sing, "Hallelujah, Worthy is the Lamb," for Christ arose from the dead for your salvation and mine.

Rose Petals

Like drops of blood
They fell upon the ground,
The petals of the crimson rose
within my hand.
Their life is over and I understand
What beauty they have given
to this land.
I saw no suffering in this symbol here,

The thorns were not at fault
for the release of life
from the exquisite flower.

But on the brow of my Eternal King
Who has the Glory and the Mighty Power
The thorns caused drops of blood
to form a ring,
And oh! the agony of death
He there endured!
With which my peace and pardon
He secured!

Easter

Our family's Easter celebrations have always been special for me. Just having them all come home with the happy voices and smiling faces is reward enough for parents. I think I have been especially blessed with a great, deep, and tender love for my children, grandchildren, and great-grandchildren. It's a love that comes from a deep well—a flow that can never be quenched—and I thank the Lord for entrusting that to me.

As you know, I am also very traditional, so before Easter comes a time to bake *paska*. In all shapes and sizes: egg-shaped and wonderfully decorated with all colors of frosting and sprinkles. Rich with butter and golden moist with eggs. Some in the shape of overgrown mushrooms, with frosting dribbling down the sides, to say nothing of the ones that never make it to the decorating stage but get eaten in huge, thick slices still warm enough to melt the butter on them. We shared this pleasure with many a neighbor's child.

Another Easter memory is the famous ham and potato salad—well-laced with onions. Homemade "hot" mustard for the ham, *zwieback*, and of course cherry *mouss*. And how I love all the planning and preparing.

In our home, music played a big role. Dietrich always directed a church choir, and I was his faithful helpmate—always ready to sing. So Easter mornings in Kansas and California always began with a sunrise service. The most glorious feeling—rhapsodic—early morning filled with excitement, watching the sunrise, seeing the people come, hearing the people greet each other with "Christ is risen," and the reply, "He is risen, indeed." And the singing, outdoors, with the birdlings helping with their cheerful notes.

The church service that followed was in a more majestic mood. Wonderful anthems that were challenging and uplifting. The resurrection story proclaimed eloquently with great joy and fervor.

And, of course, being up in the choir loft we could get a marvelous overview of all the new Easter bonnets and colorful outfits—also a type of tradition.

Rick's Accident

Rick was a student at Fresno Pacific College in 1983-84. Dietrich and I lived near the college at that time, so we enjoyed his company whenever we could, and he enjoyed a change from cafeteria food once in a while. Since his parents, Walt and Dolly, lived in Lodi, which is a two hour drive from Fresno, we were privileged to have him come "home" to us.

On January 20, 1984, Rick and his fellow student Chris Walsh went skiing. It was there that Rick had an accident by landing wrong after his jump. When Chris looked back, he saw Rick crumpled and unconscious in the snow. Right behind Rick, coming down the same slope, were a doctor and fireman. When they saw Rick helpless, they immediately gave him artificial respiration. Rick came back to pulse and breath. These men were truly a Godsend.

Minutes later, Rick was flown to St. Agnes Hospital in Fresno by helicopter, a distance of about 100 miles.

Wally and Dolly were notified at their jobs in Lodi and Sacramento. Meanwhile, our family made their way to the hospital to be with Rick.

Wally and Dolly stayed with Rick night and day, and the entire Fresno family spent as much time with him as possible.

It was a most tragic and traumatic time, for Rick was paralyzed from his neck down.

On January 22, Rick started therapy, and after ten days he was moved to Fresno Community Hospital Rehabilitation Center. Rick could not even sit without support—a heartbreaking scene!

On February 15, they took bone from Rick's hip and fused the second vertebrae onto the first one. Rick lost 25 pounds during this whole episode. When he could enjoy food again, we all made sure there was always a supply of his favorites.

Rick's classmates surrounded him with prayer and encouragement during his long hospital stay. Dozens and dozens of get well cards were pinned to the walls, and gifts of all kinds—flowers, plants, and candy filled every available place.

Wally and Dolly stayed in Fresno for a month. Then, in six weeks, they were able to take Rick to Lodi and from there to Stockton for further therapy.

Rick has recovered completely and is skiing again. It is a miracle, a total answer to many, many prayers and the support of family and friends.

*

For Rick, the Aftermath

> *Rick speaks:*
> *The whiteness of the snow*
> *Just seemed to end.*

Could white and black thus blend?
I did not know.

The ecstasy of speed
Had been so great.
Was this then fate?
Did I not heed?

The hill was smooth and long,
The snow so slick,
My pain so thick.
What was wrong?

I heard the noise of blades
And being borne aloft—somehow
The color comes and fades
The touch of loving hands on my hot brow.

And silently I cried, Dear Lord,
You are the great physician, be Thou near.
Let me believe your written word,
Do not allow my heart to fear.

And then through days and nights of pain and pills
In and out of hazy, painful dreams
With hopes that will be the end of all my ills
I suffer agony of heart and mind, or so it seems.

But then I feel a strength I do not comprehend,
Surrounding and uplifting like strong arms
A wall of prayer without beginning without end
To quiet all my fears, end my alarm.

Grandma speaks:
I saw a tear steal down your cheek,
I could not bear to wipe it dry.
My heart could only speak
A prayer to God on high.

Rick speaks:
Excruciating pain, I could not bear,
But there was help nearby.
Such comfort I derived from those who care,
I praise the Lord on high.

Flute and Cello

Sprays of silver sound float to the lofty ceiling;

Trills sparkle in the candlelight.

Velvet tones of the cello blend with the dust of the old chapel.

The music tumbles and soars like mighty waves on a restless
ocean.

The old woman sits enchanted, dreaming and reflecting. She is being carried into a realm of ethereal ecstasy!

The cello leads in volumes of deep-throated melody.

The flute hovers lightly as a summer cloud.

Suddenly, a cacophony of sound, of birds in colorful array, joyously their morning! Then ever so softly, they face into the heavenward distance; and only the three candles and one lamp remain. The candles flicker, making faint shadows.

The old woman's white hair shimmers in the pale light. Her head is bowed, her eyes are closed now, her work-worn hands still and folded.

Then a melody begins, strong and familiar, out of the past. "A Mighty Fortress is our God." So many years this has been her strength and shield!

The music swells, silver and velvet form a strong bond. "A bulwark never failing." She sings the words feebly, overcome with emotion. Very softly now the flute, thin and silky, the cello, supporting rich and firm.

Echoes "His Kingdom is Forever."

*

Final Thoughts

As I complete this memoir, I am approaching my 80th birthday. I am the mother of six children, mother-in-law to one son-in-law and five daughters-in-law, and have 16 grandchildren and 5 great-grandchildren, all of whom I love most dearly.

I have lived in many countries, provinces, states, towns, and cities, and hold dear in my memory bank and heart the countless friends I have made and lessons I have gleaned from each era and place.

There are sweet tidbits of childhood, teen years, and sentimentally romantic dreams of a Prince Charming in my future. I married that "Prince" at age nineteen, and we enjoyed a long life (fifty-one and a half years) together raising a loving family in our home filled with plentiful music and song.

I also had dreams of a higher education. However, that school for me had no desks, departments, or a graduation. I learned from the schools of life, circumstances, environment, people, the Bible, and books. These were my "halls of learning" until I was in my mid-seventies, when I had the privilege of attending writing classes at Fresno Pacific College taught by Luetta Reimer, and poetry classes taught by my well-known cousin Jean Janzen. These teachers infused me with such a magnitude of inspiration to write—inspiration to which I ascribe the writing of these memoirs.

All my life I have loved people from all walks of life. I seem to need people to prove love to them.

I leave this legacy of love to each of you who will read this: My prayer is that you would acknowledge Jesus as your Savior and be stirred to love more abundantly, to forgive more freely, and show more concern for others, for there is a world full of unloved people who are hurting. By this, we together can make a wonderful contribution and receive the crown of glory!

My arms around you.

With love, Anne

*

Prayer

May the Lord keep you
In all your ways:

Sweet in a sour place,
Cool in a hot place,

Quiet in a noisy place,
Clean in a dirty place,

Kept by His Grace—
Everywhere!

*

NINETEEN

Recipes

❃

Cookbook Musings

Bless this food Thou dids't provide,
We see Thy grace on every side.
For bounteous gift our hearts we lift
And thank Thee for Thy faithful care.

Manna from heaven we receive day by day,
Without God's blessings there is no way.
We enjoy countless blessings together, don't we?
All because manna from Heaven we see.

❃

Soup

A kettle of soup simmered long and slow,
Its flavor we greatly anticipate.
Fresh vegetables from gardens row.
We all give thanks and participate.

Chicken Noodle Soup

Broth:

Place as large a stewing hen as you can find in a large kettle, cover with water.

Add enough (2 handfuls) salt and 3 or 4 bay leaves.

Bring to boil, skim off foam, cover, and simmer for about 3 hours.

Taste, then add pepper and chicken stock base until you have good flavor.

Remove meat from bones, cut into bite-sized pieces and return to soup.

Noodles:

Slightly beat 5 whole eggs with a fork in a large bowl.

Slowly add Wonder Flour until you have a soft dough.

When too stiff to mix with fork, work with hands, gradually adding more flour until you are able to handle dough.

Sprinkle flour on board, and take a fifth of the dough and roll with rolling pin, turning dough often and adding more flour as needed until dough is very thin.

Spread on clean cloth and let dry, turning often.

Repeat with remaining dough.

When almost dry, roll each piece up and cut very thin with sharp paring knife.

Never use butcher knife. I did once and cut off my fingernail!

Cherry Mouss

My own invention—best with sweet, red Lodi cherries.

½ kettle cherries

Cover with water and bring to boil.

Add 1½-2 cups sugar.

Simmer until cherries are cooked.

Mix about 4 tbsp cornstarch with cold water and add slowly to boiling *mouss.*

Remove from heat and add 1 package cherry Jell-O, stirring well.

Cool and refrigerate.

Sugar and cornstarch amounts will vary per amount of *mouss* made.

*

The Casserole

A mother doesn't always know
How far the ingredients will actually go.
She's always looking for ways to stretch,
So the casserole dish she runs to fetch.

What mystery is hidden in this casserole?
Should it be served in plate or bowl?
Let's see, I'll try the fork—or spoon?
If it's too thin, I'll know real soon.

Methinks I taste last Sunday's roast,
Saturday's carrots and Friday's toast,
Potatoes and onions, cream and cheese,
What happened to Monday's leftover peas?

Wednesday's and Thursday's ingredients
Must not have been expedient
To put into this week's casserole,
For me to eat out of plate or bowl.

A mother's a genius, of this I will boast,
She almost disguised last Sunday's roast.
I trust it's awhile before next I see
A mysterious casserole looking up at me!

*

Wally's Macaroni

This is only good if you've never had anything better! And very inexpensive. In those "good old days," it was a weekly treat.

One enormous pot of macaroni

One large can tomatoes

Cook macaroni.

Add tomatoes.

Salt and pepper to taste.

Grandma's "Sugar Plum" Braids

This has been a great favorite in our family ever since Wally was a little boy. I try to have some on hand at all times. These are good for Easter, birthdays, 4th of July, Christmas, and Thanksgiving. If you should ever have extra, they are excellent warmed up for breakfast. I usually triple this recipe!

3½ cups flour

1 tsp salt

1 cup margarine

Prepare as for pie pastry.

Dissolve 1 package yeast in ¼ cup warm water.

¾ cup sour cream or canned milk

2 eggs, beaten

1 cup sugar (for rolling out)

Mix all ingredients, except sugar, in a large bowl. Stir with wooden spoon until well-mixed. Cover and refrigerate overnight, or 3 to 4 hours.

Sprinkle sugar on board (no flour).

Take about 1/3 of the dough and place on sugar.

Put more sugar on top of dough.

Roll with rolling pin a few times.

Add more sugar and fold dough over to center.

Roll again.

Repeat with more sugar and more rolling.

When dough is about ¼-inch thick and you have folded it about 4 or 5 times, cut into ½-inch strips and braid.

Place on cookie sheet lined with parchment paper.

Bake immediately at 375 degrees. Watch carefully so bottoms won't get too brown.

When braids are nicely browned, about 15 minutes, remove immediately from baking sheet using a spatula.

Place upside-down on waxed paper until cool.

Frost with powdered sugar glaze.

New Year's Portzelky

This is the recipe I have used since 1949—and it has never been a disaster. I still double the amount and have enough to freeze. Then there was the time I was frying these and Vic came in with about six friends—the Vogt twins, Morris Nord, and several others from college. They must have had a contest, because they cleaned me right out of portzelky. Bet you can't eat just one!

2 or 3 packages yeast, or a big chunk of Baker's yeast

dissolved in ½ cup warm water

3 cups warm milk

3 eggs, beaten

3 tbsp sugar

3 tbsp shortening

2 tsp salt

About 6 cups raisins

Enough flour to make a batter that will sort of fall from the spoon

Be sure to add flour gradually. You can always add more, but you can't take it away.

If the batter is runny, it will absorb too much oil in cooking.

In a large, deep kettle, heat about half a gallon of cooking oil.

Drop batter in by the tablespoon.

Cook about 2 to 3 minutes.

Place on paper towel on cookie sheet.

If desired, roll in sugar.

*

Holiday Preparations

The air is filled
With excitement sweet,
We think about love ones
We will meet.

Baking is done
And all is prepared
Remembering holidays we have shared.

❀

Easter Paska

Easter is paska, warm and brown,
Frosting and sprinkles is their crown;
They stand like sentries tall and straight,
Symbols of rising from death's dark gate

❀

Paska

6 packages yeast
¾ cup warm water
1 tbsp sugar
Dissolve yeast and sugar in water.

4½ cups milk, part canned milk
3 cups sugar
3 cups margarine, melted 4 tsp salt
4 tsp vanilla
7 eggs, beaten
Flour

Warm the milk.
Add the sugar, stirring to dissolve.

In large bowl, mix 3 to 4 cups flour, milk, and sugar mixture, salt, vanilla, eggs, yeast mixture, and melted butter.

Mix well with wooden spoon.

Gradually add more flour until you have to knead by hand.

Dough should be moderately stiff, slightly sticky.

Knead until smooth.

Cover and let rise in warm place until very light.

Grease 1 or 2 pound coffee cans, or any pans used, with shortening.

Fill half full with dough and cover.

Let rise until double.

Bake at 300 degrees for 25 to 30 minutes.

If it gets too brown, cover with brown paper and bake until done.

Frost when cooled.

Frosting:

Mix together powdered sugar, melted margarine, water, and vanilla.

Verenika

Cottage cheese filling:

1 package dry cottage cheese

1 tsp salt

Crumble cheese thoroughly with hands in a large mixing bowl.

Add 3 or 4 egg yolks and mix well until smooth, patting down firmly with back of spoon.

Cherry filling:

Use pitted cherries with 1 tsp sugar per square.

Dough:

3 or 4 egg whites
1 tsp salt
1 cup milk
4 cups flour
1 tsp baking powder
½ cup oil

Add the flour gradually to eggs and milk (may require more or less). Dough should be firm.

Knead a few minutes on floured board, then divide into small pieces and roll out carefully on floured (not too much flour) board, lifting and turning several times.

When thin enough, cut into 4-inch squares.

Place 1 tbsp cottage cheese mixture in center and pinch edges.

Lay on floured cookie sheet.

When all are made, boil 6 to 8 *verenika* in a large kettle of salted water.

Boil about 4 minutes.

Place verenika in a pan with melted butter to coat.

Remove and place in serving dish.

Gravy:

Melt butter in frying pan.

Add canned milk, ham or sausage drippings, and sour cream.

Do not bring to a boil after adding sour cream, as it will curdle.

If gravy is too thick, add milk to thin.

Turkey Dressing

I have made this since our first year in Hillsboro—Christmas 1950.

Bread crumbs (equivalent to one package store-bought bread cubes)

2 eggs

½ cup margarine, melted

2 cups celery, finely chopped

1 medium onion

Salt, pepper, poultry seasoning, to taste

Enough milk, water or stock to make a moist dressing that will keep its shape when you squeeze a handful (add gradually so as not to add too much)

*

Bread

The tantalizing smell of bread,
Hot from the oven and thickly spread,
With butter that melts on crunchy crust,
More than one loaf is a definite "must."

Manna from heaven we receive day by day,
Without God's blessing there is no way.
We enjoy bounteous blessings together, don't we?
All because manna from heaven we see.

*

Brown Bread

This is my own concoction and it has always been eaten—hot or cold.

¼ package Kellogg's All-Bran cereal

2 or 3 cups whole wheat flour

3 cups hot water

2 packages Fleischman's yeast

½ cup warm water

1 tsp sugar

Dissolve yeast and sugar in water.

1½ tsp salt

Flour, enough to make a stiff dough

Pour All-Bran into a large bowl.

Pour the hot water over the bran.

When cooled to lukewarm, add yeast.

Stir until dissolved.

Add salt and whole wheat flour.

Mix and add white flour.

Stir with spoon until it gets too heavy.

Then add a little flour at a time and knead with hands until smooth.

Grease loaf pans with shortening.

Divide dough and place in pans.

Cover with towel and let raise until slightly over the top of pan.

Bake at 400 degrees for 40 minutes.

Remove from pan and cool.

French Bread

1 package yeast

1 tbsp sugar

1½ cups lukewarm water

Dissolve yeast and sugar in water.

4 cups flour (no need to sift)

2 tsp salt

Add flour to liquid.

Mix until sticky.

Cover and let rise, about 30-45 minutes.

Turn out onto floured foil (it will be somewhat sticky).

Put in well-greased (with shortening) 2-quart casserole.

Let raise until it comes to top of bowl—about 1 hour.

Bake at 400 degrees for 35 minutes.

Remove from bowl.

Brush with butter.

Serve hot.

Sweet Rolls—Butter Horns

3 packages dry yeast

½ cup warm water

Dissolve yeast in water.

3 cups milk, scalded

¾ cup sugar

3 tsp salt

Add to milk.

Stir until dissolved.

1 cup shortening, melted (can be half margarine)

Pour lukewarm milk mixture into large bowl.

Add shortening and 3 eggs.

Gradually add flour (about 10 cups) until not too sticky.

Knead by hand until smooth.

Cover and let rise until double.

Punch down, let rise.

Shape into desired rolls.

Let rise on pan.

Brush with melted butter.

Bake at 400 degrees for 12 to 15 minutes.

Makes about 4 to 5 dozen.

Variations

Raisin bread:

Using sweet roll dough, add 4 cups raisins.

Cinnamon rolls:

Roll out a piece of dough 16 by 10 inches.

Spread with melted butter.

Sprinkle generously with cinnamon and 3 to 4 tbsp white sugar.

Roll up as a jelly roll.

Cut into 1-inch pieces.

Place on well-greased pan.

Bake 25 minutes.

Remove from pan and drizzle with glaze.

For glaze, make a soft paste of powdered sugar and water.

Gooey top:

In pie pan, place enough brown sugar to cover bottom.

Drizzle melted butter over sugar.

Place the cut cinnamon rolls on top.

Let rise.

Bake.

Remove at once, turning upside-down on plate.

Cinnamon Bread:

Pinch off a piece of dough, enough for a small loaf.

Roll into a long, narrow piece about the length of a bread board.

Brush entire length of dough with water.

Sprinkle generously with cinnamon.

Roll up to form a loaf.

Put in greased bread pan.

Let rise.

Slash top before baking.

Bake at 350 degrees for 40 minutes.

Christmas Bread

These various breads are from my own recipe, laboriously tried and tested, measured and re-measured after our move to California. The soft wheat flour was so different from the Canadian hard wheat. It was tested and approved, finally, by such experts as Dietrich, Kathy, Walter, Vic, and Allan. The other two members accepted the above without question!

Add raisins, chopped glazed fruit.

Take out three balls of dough and make each one into a long rope.

Braid rope and place on greased cookie sheet.

Let rise.

Bake.

Drizzle with glaze.

Three Loaves of Brown Bread

By Milt, May 19, 1984 in White Plains, New York
Milton and I made this bread—we had so much fun in his
primitive, little kitchen. He composed the recipe—the bread
was delicious!

Put in some bran (that's what I do at home). After much consternation, add 3 cups water (warm).

(For two loaves, use less of both—consternation and water.)

Add dissolved yeast.

3 tsp salt

1½ cups whole wheat flour

2½ – 3 cups white flour

¼ cup vegetable oil

Add flour gradually until kneadable, then talk about losing and finding a small diamond.

Add a little more oil, kneading the whole while, till you can play catch with it. Be on the lookout for not-stickiness.

Plop dough into Crisco-ized pans. Use coffee cans if you want. Remember the old adage, "Early to bread; early to rise."

Go away for an hour. Bake at 400 degrees for 40 minutes or 12,000 miles!

❋

Stew

A bubbling pot of stew, delicious—hot
From days of yore—I've not forgot
With homemade bread you sop the plate
And look for more upon the grate.

❋

Zwieback

This is the amount I have baked all these years. It was always so much fun to bake for all my children!

1 large chunk of Baker's yeast

¾ cup warm water

1 tbsp sugar

Dissolve yeast and sugar in water.

6 cups milk, warmed

1 cup shortening, melted

½ cup margarine, melted

4 tsp salt

Flour

Sift part of the flour into a large bowl.

Add milk, salt and yeast mixture to flour, stirring with wooden spoon until smooth.

Add melted shortening, stirring until smooth.

Gradually keep adding more sifted flour.

Knead until smooth (dough should not be sticky).

Cover and let rise until very light.

Grease hands slightly and form into *zwieback*, placing on baking sheet.

Let rise.

Bake at 400 degrees for 15 to 20 minutes.

❋

Cake

As soft and light as a summer's cloud,
One thick slice will be allowed,
To cover with berries and whipped up cream,
The answer to everyone's favorite dream.

❋

Sister Mary's Graham Cracker Cake

Line a 9 x 13-inch pan with 15 whole graham crackers.

1 cup brown sugar

½ cup butter

½ cup milk

Cook together.

Remove from heat.

1 cup crushed graham crackers

1 cup coconut

1 cup walnuts

Add to sugar mixture.

Mix well and pour over crackers in pan (mixture will be thick).

Cover with 15 whole graham crackers.

Spread with vanilla frosting.

Sprinkle with chopped nuts.

Ready to eat—no baking!

Danish Coffee Cake

Pastry:

1 package Fleischman's yeast

½ cup plus 2 tbsp water

1 tbsp sugar

Dissolve yeast and sugar in water.

2½ cups flour

½ tsp salt

Mix flour and salt.

1 cup margarine, chilled

1 egg, beat well

Grate margarine into flour mixture and rub together to make coarse crumbs.

Add dissolved yeast and egg.

Mix with wooden spoon.

Cover and chill 2 hours or overnight.

Roll pastry on floured board to fit 11x17-inch cookie sheet.

Bring up sides slightly.

Pour 21-ounce can Comstock cherry pie filling on pastry and distribute evenly.

Cover with topping crumbs. Bake at 375 degrees until

golden brown and pulled away from sides—25-35 minutes.

Crumb topping:
>9 tbsp flour
>9 tbsp sugar
>6 tbsp margarine
>Mix into crumb mixture.

﹡

Cookies

>*I stir and mix the cookie dough.*
>*I form the cookies row by row.*
>*I bake them warmly, not in haste,*
>*And serve them prettily for all to taste.*

﹡

World's Best Cookies

1 cup margarine
1 cup white sugar
1 cup brown sugar
1 egg
1 cup oil
1 cup rolled oats
1 cup crushed corn flakes
½ cup shredded coconut
½ cup chopped walnuts
3½ cups flour

1 tsp soda

1 tsp salt

1 tsp vanilla

Cream margarine and sugars.

Add egg and beat until fluffy.

Add oil and mix well.

Add all other ingredients and mix well.

Form into walnut-sized balls on cookie sheet.

Press down with fork.

Bake at 325 degrees for 12 minutes.

Makes 6 to 7 dozen.

Pepper Nuts

Pepper Nuts made with Anne's recipe, Chrismas 2010

1 cup shortening

1 cup white sugar

1 cup brown sugar

2 eggs

½ tsp allspice

½ tsp ginger

1 tsp baking soda

1 – 1½ tsp pepper

½ cup cold coffee

5 cups flour

Mix well.

Form into small balls and shape into pencil-thin rope and place ropes on cookie sheet in freezer to harden (makes

is good) pieces.

l lightly browned, 10 to 12

Add ½ tsp anise oil

-or-

Replace cold coffee with 2 tbsp instant coffee (This will give you a crisper cookie, and a very good one!).

◈

"I'm home, Mom!" from the kitchen door
Comes the shout every day at four.
Milk and cookies, or what will it be
That Mom has with love prepared for me?

◈

Ammonia Cookies

I don't think we could have Christmas without these!

1 cup melted shortening

1½ cup white sugar

1 cup sour cream

2 eggs

1 tsp soda

3 tsp powdered ammonia dissolved in 3 tbsp boiling water

1 tsp peppermint flavoring

Flour

Mix in order given, adding 3 cups flour.

Continue mixing and adding more flour—3 more cups, according to how hard the dough gets.

The dough is rich, so is not difficult to handle. The dough must be soft.

Pat out on well-floured board.

Roll about ½-inch thick.

Cut out small cookies, as they grow quite a bit.

Place far apart on cookie sheet.

Bake at 325 degrees about 10 minutes.

Cookies must not get brown.

When cool, mix powdered sugar.

Frosting:

Mix powdered sugar with a little melted butter and water to make a soft frosting.

Add a few drops of peppermint flavoring.

Spread on cooled cookies.

Store in tightly closed container.

Cowboy Cookies

1 cup margarine

1 cup white sugar

1 cup brown sugar

2 eggs

2 cups flour

1 tsp baking soda

½ tsp salt

½ tsp baking powder

1 tsp vanilla

1 12-oz package chocolate chips

1 cup old-fashioned oats

1 cup quick oats

(It is absolutely necessary to use BOTH kinds of oats!)

Bake at 350 degrees for 15 minutes.

Pastry

(For Butter Tarts and Platz)

From Five Roses Cookbook, Lake of the Woods, Montreal, Canada and Winnipeg, Canada, 1938.

It was always my assignment to bring these to our summer outings at Granite Lake with the Victor Wilms and John DeFehrs. Somehow, there were never any left to bring home!

3 cups flour

1 cup lard, or shortening, or shortening and margarine

1 tsp baking powder

1 scant cup cold water

Dissolve baking powder in water.

Mix as for pastry, adding water gradually until dough forms a ball.

Roll on floured board.

Butter Tart Filling:

    1/3 cup butter

    2 tbsp cream, or milk

    1 egg, beaten

    1 cup brown sugar

    1 cup raisins

    1 tsp vanilla

Wash raisins and heat in water to simmer, just a few minutes.

    Drain.

    Add other ingredients and mix well.

    Place spoonful in pastry-lined muffin pan.

    Bake at 450 degrees for 8 minutes.

Reduce heat to 350 degrees and bake until pastry is delicately brown.

Fresh Fruit Filling for Platz or Perishki:

    Apples, chopped, or halved apricots

    Sugar

    Flour

    Roll dough in large piece.

    Cut into five-inch strips.

    Place fruit down center of strip.

    Sprinkle generously with sugar and flour.

    Wet edge of dough with water and pinch edges together.

    Place on cookie sheet, pinched side up.

    Bake at 400 degrees until well-browned.

Meat Pereshki

Dough:

Use sweet roll dough (see "Sweet Roll" recipe) with sugar cut down to ½ cup.

Pinch off small piece of dough as for bottom of *zwieback.*

Flatten out on floured board until size of a large cookie.

Put in a spoonful of meat filling.

Pinch edges down on cookie sheet.

Bake immediately at 375 degrees.

Meat filling:

1 lb. lean ground beef

1 small onion

Salt and pepper

Mix together.

Sauté gently.

Add 2 hard-boiled eggs, chopped.

Cool.

Glaze:

Brush each piece of dough with melted butter

-or-

1 egg, slightly beaten and 1 tbsp water

Roll Kuchen

Aunt Mary's recipe

5 eggs, slightly beaten

1 cup sour cream

½ cup milk

2 tsp baking powder

1 tsp baking soda

1½ tsp salt

Flour

Add sour cream, milk, some flour, and dry ingredients to eggs.

Add more flour gradually until dough shapes so you can put it on floured board, and work a little more flour into it.

Divide dough into small pieces.

Roll each piece until ¼-inch thick.

Cut into strips 3 inches wide and then into 4-inch lengths.

Cut slit in middle and pull one end through slit.

Fry in deep hot fat—they will fry quickly.

Turn once and remove to paper towel-lined platter when brown.

This makes a large amount. You may want to cut recipe in half.

Variation:

This is also very delicious with a spoonful of prepared

meat (see "Meat Pereshki" recipe) placed in each square of dough. Pinch edges and fry exactly as for Roll Kuchen.

❧

"Better is a dish of vegetables where love is
Than a fattened ox and hatred with it."
—*Proverbs 15:17*

❧

Borscht

1 small chuck roast, or 1 package stewing beef

3 quarts water

Salt to taste

Bring meat to boil and skim foam as it comes to the top.

Cover and boil gently until meat is done.

Remove meat, cool and shred or cut into bite-sized pieces.

Add to broth in order given:

Several sprigs of fresh dill, or 2 tsp dried dill weed

2 chopped onions

4 to 5 chopped carrots

Several ribs of celery (optional)

1 medium head of cabbage, chopped

Cook until vegetables are tender.

Add 1 can (20 oz) of tomatoes.

Add the meat and simmer for about 20 minutes.

Add salt and pepper as needed.

This is delicious served with French Bread recipe.

Russian Pancakes, or Big Pancakes

Mix in large bowl:

>   3 cups flour
>
>   1½ tsp salt
>
>   1 tbsp sugar
>
>   Stir in about 2 cups milk.

Add 3 or 4 whole eggs and mix well, adding more milk gradually until batter is thin enough to run off ladle.

Heat skillet.

Add a little oil and pour batter in skillet to cover bottom.

When light brown on bottom, turn over and brown other side.

Remove to plate.

As you bake, add oil for each pancake.

Makes approximately 15 to 20 pancakes.

These are delicious served with boysenberry sauce and powdered sugar.

Sauce:

>   2 to 3 cups fresh or frozen boysenberries
>
>   ¾ cups sugar
>
>   ½ cup water

Simmer gently and thicken with corn starch paste. Serve warm.

I DO hope you can get some use out of these recipes. I have enjoyed them for so many years. I had done very little baking before I was married, but it was a great challenge and source of satisfaction when things turned out happily.

❋

My cup runneth over by God's good grace
measure by measure in every place
His watchful eye knows all my needs
From His own hand, He daily feeds

❋

And now, Happy Eating!

TWENTY

Epilogue

In the early fall of 1996, I was given the opportunity to go to Ukraine, the country where I was born and lived the first eight years of my life.

I will not forget the wonderful renewal I felt walking along the streets of the Mennonite villages, seeing the houses, barns, churches, schools, hospitals, and factories that our forefathers built.

To me, it was my life coming full circle, the fulfillment of a journey I began 80 years ago. When I returned home from my motherland, I wrote the poem "A Song of the Molotschna Colony," which is an appropriate ending to these memoirs.

"Remove not the ancient landmarks which thy fathers have set."

—Proverbs 22: 28

Good bless you and keep you.

A Song of the Molotschna Colony
Anne Friesen, 1996

The streets of the villages no longer looked
well-groomed as they had in the distant past.
The grape arbors and trees
were overgrown and neglected,
doors and gates hung askew.

Geese, ducks, and chickens
roamed freely across
yard and garden,
intent on finding a kernel
here and there,
goats were tethered and feeding
on scanty patches of green.

When Mrs. Pankratz told us her story
of how she suffered
through the bitter years
of war and revolution,
of hatred, cruelty, and murder,
we were reminded of the
terrible tragedies of the old world
that many of us had also experienced.

Sadness, heartache, and sympathy
burned in our hearts,
mingled with salty tears
when in parting we joined
our voices and sang:
"Gott ist die Liebe"
and had the assurance that
our gracious and Almighty God
had not forsaken us.

Praise His Name.

The End

Editor's Note

to the Second Printing

With Love, Anne was first published for the eightieth birthday of Anne Friesen, taking place on March 17, 1997. At the festive celebration the Friesen family held for her that year at Butler Mennonite Church in Fresno, California, Anne sat at a table and proudly signed copies of her memoir for an eager audience.

Only 100 copies of *With Love, Anne* were printed at that time. A few Mennonite historical libraries asked for copies, finding archival significance in the story of a young Mennonite girl's journey from the Russian Steppes to America, but there were not enough books to go around. Now, with the advantage of on-demand printing, the family is pleased to be able to make *With Love, Anne* available once again.

Anne lived an additional thirteen years after publication of her book, dying in Fresno, California, on September 3, 2010, at the age of 93. During those years, there were additions to Anne's lineage, some family deaths, and many celebrations and holidays that family and friends were able to share in the presence of this great matriarch. For this second printing of *With Love, Anne*, we have updated the "List of Descendants," but all other words remain purely hers.

As an historical document, *With Love, Anne* is a photograph of a life bridging two worlds: the Mennonites in Russia, and the immigrant life in North America. As a memoir, the book is a lasting memory of Anne for those who knew and loved her, as well as those who never met her but owe their existence to her; namely, her descendants.

Anne's final years found her as cheerful and well-coiffed as she had always been. She certainly "showed her years," but were you to have visited her in her tiny but typically Anne-outfitted apartment during that time, you would most likely have found yourself not alone, because she never stopped receiving friends, family, and guests into her generous, loving world.

My grandma loved books. She nurtured this love in me from the time I was born, as she always told me, holding me in her arms and reading to me. It is due to her that today I make books for a living, and she is in each word of every one.

Our last words to each other were, "I love you forever," a phrase with which we had always ended our times together.

Randall Friesen
2016

List of Descendants

～

Dietrich Friesen
b. January 11, 1914; d. February 28, 1988

Anne (Warkentin) **Friesen**
b. March 17, 1917; d. September 3, 2010

Married October 22, 1936

(Anne Friesen made no distinction between adopted, step, or birth children. To her, every member of her family was equally loved and equally part of her heritage and history. But for purposes of this list as an historical document, these categories have been noted. The list has also been updated for this current edition.)

Katherine Rosamund (Friesen) **Goertzen/Robinson**
b. July 9, 1937; d. July 26, 2006
    Diana Lynn (Goertzen) Douglass, b. January 10, 1960
        Justin Nathaniel Douglass, b. November 23, 1980
            Emery Douglass, b.September 1, 2007
        Branden Ryan Douglass, b. July 3, 1983
            Jedadiah Douglass (adopted), b. July 8, 2009
            Wilhelm Douglass, b. November 9, 2015
        Marissa Katherine Elizabeth Douglass,
        b. July 22, 1994
    Brian Goertzen, b. March 25, 1963
        Emily Braun (Goertzen) Alvarado,
        b. October 29, 1986
            Roman Alavarado, b. April 4, 2014
        Chelsea Braun (Goertzen) DeBennedetto,
        b. August 23, 1989
            Baer DeBennedetto, b. April 21, 2015

Walter Herbert Friesen
b. October 2, 1939; d. August 21, 2015
    Randall Scott Friesen, b. April 22, 1962
    Richard Todd Friesen, b. June 11, 1964
        Pepper Elizabeth Friesen, b. January 13, 1998

Victor Emmanuel Friesen
b. December 18, 1941; d. July 4, 2007
    Peter Contino Friesen (adopted), b. October 8, 1965

Allan Orlando Friesen
b. October 24, 1946

    Jason Ford (step-son), b. April 8, 1972

        Riley Ford, b. January 15, 2006

        Milo Ford, b. February 19, 2009

    Samantha (Ford) Heinl (step-daughter),
b. September 25, 1973

        Sydney Heinl, b. October 26, 2004

        Lucas Heinl, b. March 28, 2007

    Sara Renee Friesen, b June 13, 1983

    Addison Allan Friesen, b. April 1, 1986

Eugene Mark Friesen
b. February 17, 1952

    Anna James (Percival) Miller, b. June 11, 1983

    Zoe Rose Friesen, b. May 30, 1986

    Noel Benjamin Friesen, b. October 15, 1991

    Elliott Lee Friesen, b. February 4, 1994

    Lily Doris Huitong Friesen (adopted),
b. February 20, 2001

    Katherine Lorraine Changgao Friesen (adopted),
b. May 3, 2001

Milton James Friesen
b. May 11, 1954

    Analiese Meg (Friesen) Domingos,
b. September 6, 1983

Christian Domingos, b. February 16, 2015

Evan Baird (step-son), b. December 25, 1985

Reese Baird, b. October 18, 2013

Easton Baird, b. July 24, 2015

Carsten Dietrich Friesen, b. February 22, 1991

Made in the USA
Charleston, SC
08 May 2016